CULTURAL

STUDIES

Volume 3   Number 1   January 1989

T0373661

CULTURAL STUDIES is a new international journal, dedicated to the notion that the study of cultural processes, and especially of popular culture, is important, complex, and both theoretically and politically rewarding. It is published three times a year, with issues being edited in rotation from Australia, the UK and the USA, though occasional issues will be edited from elsewhere. Its international editorial collective consists of scholars representing the range of the most influential disciplinary and theoretical approaches to cultural studies.

CULTURAL STUDIES will be in the vanguard of developments in the area worldwide, putting academics, researchers, students and practitioners in different countries and from diverse intellectual traditions in touch with each other and each other's work. Its lively international dialogue will take the form not only of scholarly research and discourse, but also of new forms of writing, photo essays, cultural reviews and political interventions.

CULTURAL STUDIES will publish articles on those practices, texts and cultural domains within which the various social groups that constitute a late capitalist society negotiate patterns of power and meaning. It will engage with the interplay between the personal and the political, between strategies of domination and resistance, between meaning systems and social systems.

CULTURAL STUDIES will seek to develop and transform those perspectives which have traditionally informed the field — structuralism and semiotics, Marxism, psychoanalysis and feminism. Theories of discourse, of power, of pleasure and of the institutionalization of meaning are crucial to its enterprise; so too are those which stress the ethnography of culture.

Contributions should be sent to either the General Editor or one of the Associate Editors. They should be in duplicate and should conform to the reference system set out in the Notes for Contributors, available from the Editors or Publishers. They make take the form of articles of about 5000 words, of kites (short, provocative or exploratory pieces) of about 2000 words, or of reviews of books, other cultural texts or events.

Advertisements: Enquiries to David Polley, Routledge,
11 New Fetter Lane, London EC4P 4EE.

Subscription Rates (calendar year only): UK and rest of the world:
individuals £22; institutions £38.50; North America: individuals $42;
institutions $63. All rates include postage. Subscriptions to: Subscriptions
Department, Routledge, North Way, Andover, Hants, SP10 5BE.

Single copies available on request.

ISSN 0950–2386

Typeset by Scarborough Typesetting Services

Transferred to Digital Printing 2004

CONTENTS

JENNIFER CRAIK

'I MUST PUT MY FACE ON': MAKING UP THE BODY AND MARKING OUT THE FEMININE

From a mere masquerade to the mask, from a role to a person, to an individual, from the last to a being with a metaphysical and ethical value, from a moral consciousness to a sacred being, from the latter to a fundamental form of thought and action – that is the route we have now covered. (Mauss, 1979:90)

Make-up in western rhetoric presents itself as an integral step on the way to realizing femininity, where femininity is a state of achievement and ascription, not a fact of biology or gender. The road to femininity is not necessarily smooth. Linda Evans 're-vealed' for example, has revealed that she was not always 'a beauty':

Dynasty's Linda Evans turned herself from a Plain Jane into a beautiful star . . . by massaging her face with honey every day and trying to stick her tongue up her nose . . . 'But I reckon most women could do what I did', she said. (Munday, 1986:13)

Femininity is a masquerade which involves masking, manipulating, and transforming the raw bodily material, apparently to the end of seduction but more pervasively in the exercise of narcissism. Consider these examples from beauty 'queens', Linda Evans and Britt Ekland.

Linda Evans' daily beauty routine is both daunting and bizarre:

Every morning before work she swims more than a kilometre in her pool, then goes through an elaborate facial exercise routine she swears has made her the beauty she is today.

1

'I avoid a double chin by opening my mouth wide and sticking my tongue out and up as far as it will go. I'd advise every woman to try it. You can feel the neck muscles tighten.

'I do it 50 times a day. Once you get past the age of 25 you cannot ignore your face – if you do, the muscles will start to sag.

'You don't have to fall apart as you get older. My face is taut only because of the exercise and massage that rubs out wrinkles. And I fully expect to be looking good at 85.

'My facial treatment works by putting the muscles under tension and flushing extra blood through them.

'For instance, I put my head down twice a day for five minutes. You can stand on your head, but all you need is to have your head lower than your feet. This ensures a good supply of blood to the facial tissues.'

Linda also covers her face in honey every day – avoiding eyes, eyebrows and hair. She reckons this cleans pores, making her skin look young and fresh.

'I leave the honey on for three minutes, then with my fingers I press in and snap out all over my face. This creates a vacuum suction effect, drawing out any debris from the pores and leaving the skin smooth.'

She also spends up to an hour a day smoothing out her laughter lines and little wrinkles. (Munday, 1986: 13)

Britt Ekland has compiled her routines as advice in a book entitled *Sensual Beauty and How To Achieve It*:

I'm a woman and I'm vain and I really don't want anyone to see me without make-up in public. I don't feel that I have to put on a pretty face for a man, although usually one does to start with. . . .

So the secret is to use make-up skilfully to achieve what I call a slightly overdone, natural look. (Ekland, 1984: 65)

Even the bedroom requires a special make-up routine designed to 'conceal blemishes' and emphasize the eyes, for 'nothing is more sensual than the bedroom-eyed look . . .' (ibid: 75). Britt's book is organized around a plethora of flattering photographs of herself amid 'practical' advice for readers-who-aren't-stars, all of which entail extensive remoulding of natural attributes. For example, Britt's make-up routine involves eighteen detailed steps to apply with additional advice for disguising 'problems' as well as for removing make-up.

Books about beauty secrets are numerous and highly lucrative. Their sales figures attest the existence of a voracious readership obsessed with finding the key to true femininity. But is this quest universal? Does the use of make-up (and body decoration more generally) always allude to displays of sexuality? Anthropologies of the body almost always concern 'primitive' societies yet are frequently evoked in analyses of western uses of make-up, clothes, and gesture. This article questions this explanatory practice arguing instead that western make-up plays a very different role from 'primitive' body decoration beyond superficial connections and borrowings.

The contrasts are highlighted in a book review by Francis Huxley which juxtaposed an anthropological study by Andrew and Marilyn Strathern, *Self-Decoration in Mount Hagen*, with Princess Pignatelli's *The Beautiful People's Beauty Book, or How to achieve the look and manner of the world's most attractive women* (M. Strathern, 1979: 241). This unusual comparison assumed that make-up could be seen to have parallel roles in 'western' and 'primitive' societies. Certainly Huxley has a point in that comparison. Anthropological accounts of body decoration (sic, *not* make-up) treat it in terms of significant social or religious functions (for example, as indicators of wealth, status, or rites of passage) or else in terms of aesthetics (as part of primitive art). It is never dealt with as 'fashion' – that is, as changing, ephemeral, and variable. The Stratherns' study of New Guinea Hagen decorations stands alone in beginning to examine head-dresses and body decoration in terms which recognize changing conventions over time and individual variation that are not only the product of structural or aesthetic forces.[1] But even though there may be some parallels between the uses of body decoration in a cosmetic mode, Marilyn Strathern suggests that the significance of patterns of usage differ in the Hagen example and western societies (see Figure 1). Whereas we are caught in the paradox that make-up enhances bodily parts while simultaneously detracting from 'our uniqueness', Hageners consciously exploit this:

> They emphasise that when as a group they dress themselves in feathers, paint and leaves, the first thing spectators should see is the decoration – so discovering the individual underneath becomes a pleasurable shock. They are not dressing up in costumes taking an animal or spirit form; they are not wearing masks, enacting myths or working out dramas. They are pretending to be no one but themselves, yet themselves decorated to the point of disguise. This idea is incorporated specifically into aesthetics: a dancer recognised at once has decorated himself poorly. (M. Strathern, 1979: 243)

Thus for the Hageners, the object of disguise is to mask identity:

> Here is a fundamental contrast with those cosmetic systems whose aim is *not disguise but enhancement* – according to prevalent style – of the actor's personal beauty. *Their focus is the particular body, whose features are regarded as a kind of resource.* (ibid, my emphasis)

The western use of make-up involves a double movement upon the body but always with the object of inscribing personality, of signifying a set of *clues* about *that individual body*, in stark contrast both with the heavily decorated Hagener whose decorations deflect attention away from the individual and with the Japanese Kabuki practice of whitening the face 'to erase all anterior trace of the features' (Barthes, 1982: 88) and render the face as 'the thing to write' through the black of the eyes alone.[2]

Our concern is both with external notions of beauty and style and internal notations of personality and individuality:

Figure 1: Parallels in primitive and western design
This New Guinea highlands head-dress (top) shows an inventiveness and range of motifs which are cannibalised in Mary Quant's 'Mid-summer Madness' face (below). Whereas New Guineans decorate to disguise themselves, Quant's face is designed to construct individuality and identity.

Cosmetics in our own culture beautify the body. Involved are aesthetic values, a sense of style and context, and the overt aim of enhancing the individual. By rendering the person in a particular style in itself beautiful, he or she too becomes more beautiful than in the unadorned state. (M. Strathern, 1979:241)

According to Andrew Strathern the impossibility of the promise of make-up hangs on a central paradox:

Make-up enhances individual attractiveness, yet it also stereotypes the individual, and it is especially women to whom the paradox applies. Why? The double character of the female gender, as both subject and object in a sexual context, underlies the paradox. (A. Strathern, 1981:35)

This paradox is especially insidious for those in the public gaze as indicated in an article which compared the features and make-up make-overs of Princess Diana and the Duchess of York:

Dazzling Diana and fabulous Fergie, royal sisters-in-law, are two of the most photographed women in the world . . . Who is the fairer of the two? . . .
The secret of their polished good looks is, of course, professional help. But, with the tricks these titled ladies use, any woman can become as poised as a Princess. . . .
Diana:
Britain's future Queen seems the typical English rose with her pink and white complexion. . . .
Now she has learned to brush soft shades of peach and coral down the sides of her face to narrow her naturally round face and play down her strong jaw.
Di's other facial flaw is her prominent roman nose. Today, she cleverly blends blusher down each side to make it less obvious, and uses the old model-girl trick of brushing a darker blusher around the tip to 'shorten' it.
In the past, she did not make the most of her enormous eyes.
Now, she uses frosted caramel, brown and rust shades. She often adds bright blue kohl pencil inside the lower lid of her eyes with, occasionally, a very thin, blue, liquid eyeliner on the top lids. . . .
Fergie:
Freckle faced Fergie never bothered much about makeup until Prince Andrew asked her to marry him. She got by with a lick of lipstick and a touch of mascara.
Now. She is a lot more conscious of her makeup needs.
She uses a thin film of foundation to disguise, but not hide, her freckles. A dusting of loose powder sets the base makeup.
Fergie has also learned to emphasise her eyes much more. She now uses liquid liner in dark brown to elongate her eyes at the outside corners. . . .
'Her eyes are deepset, so she has to make the eyelids come forward by

lightening them with an iridescent peachy-pink eyeshadow. . .'. ('Dazzling but different – the beauty secrets of Fergie and Di', *New Idea*, 14 March 1987:12–13)

The Princess of Wales Fashion Handbook formalizes the details of how Diana achieved 'the most remarkable metamorphosis on Royal record . . . virtually by herself' (James, 1984:30) where the changes are said to have transformed Diana into 'the elegant, mature and beautiful woman of today' (ibid.:35). Diana's routine is then generalized for four facial types – oval, heart, round, and square – in order to disguise certain aspects and highlight others with the aim of producing the illusion of the contemporary ideal of a modified oval (hollow-cheeked), an ideal that leads models to have their (healthy) back molars extracted. This illusion of the desirable face shape is enhanced by the accompanying sketches which use a base head that reproduces the common *perceptual* tendency to cut off the top of the head to elongate the eyes, to drop the mouth and thus to produce highly distorted facial contours: a perceptual joke that increases the impossibility of achieving the perfect face: loss of face precisely.[3]

Women have become The Face, yet their achievement of face paralyses other social practices. For as the face becomes the canvas for decoration, so femininity becomes the *product of actions* upon the body: in contrast, masculinity is a set of bodily parts and the *actions they can perform.*

In societies where men also decorate themselves, the intentions and symbolism of makeup are rather more concerned with status, power, and ritual displays, assertions of 'continuity and conformity' (A. Strathern, 1981:33); among Mount Hageners, for example,

> black face paint represents the internal group solidarity of males and their aggressiveness toward outsiders. While the bright colours of red and yellow stood for female values, sexual appeal, and intergroup friendship, affinity, and exchange. Finally . . . white mediate(s) between black and red, but (was) attributed largely to the male gender. (ibid.:26)

Explanations of body decoration in anthropological contexts reveal at least as much about the assumptions of anthropology's monocular view as about the workings of exotic societies. That view turns on the play of the term 'exotica',[4] a term which mystifies the workings of primitive societies and assumes that they are reducible to their primitivism. Judith Ennew has argued that anthropology has traditionally studied *different* peoples as others: 'as separate communities, only recently contacted, upon whom the impact of "Western" society had only recently taken effect. They were studied for the difference this brought to attention or produced' (Ennew, 1980:2).

This methodology of 'isolationism' entailed a distinction between *us* as everyday, rational, and understood as opposed to *them* who were cast as exotic, irrational, and to-be-understood. The realm of exotica (of difference, of mystery, of play) belonged to 'them' and explains our perpetual plundering of 'their' artefacts, symbols and decorations to enhance the perceived dullness and known character of 'our world' as opposed to the elusiveness of 'disappearing worlds' (terms that Ennew points out were used symptomatically as the titles of two documentary series (ibid.: 6, 9–10)).

Part of such projects, however, involves *our* obsession with retaining the disappearing world by insisting 'that the subjects discard any items of modern dress for the sake of the camera' (ibid.: 10) or only donning traditional dress and decoration to perform routines for the gaze of (paying) tourists. Ennew argues that the difficulty of presenting 'local' ('them') customs in any 'successful' way on camera has transposed 'the problem of verity on to the commentator's plausibility':

> If the commentator is credible the film is real. In a cross-cultural examination of native art, for instance, David Attenborough stated his intention to 'cross the barrier that so often conceals the meaning of tribal art from the sophisticated European eye'. What emerged was a 'primitive' version of Kenneth Clark's similar personal view of 'Civilisation'; a civilisation of the non-sophisticated. Attenborough himelf took the stance of the observer, walking beside a series of cliff-paintings as if he were in an art gallery; the demonstrator, pointing to the facets of building techniques in an Inca house; or the curator, handling an object as if it were an artefact and not, as he claimed, 'the expression of their myths and philosophies'. (ibid.: 10)

Because anthropology is organized around the production of difference, explanations of 'primitive' art take the form of demonstrations of the exotic; they have three main elements which are reflected in these explanations for facial/body decoration as:

1   merely a type of aesthetic expression where the body serves as just another kind of surface to be decorated;
2   an allusion to aspects of social structure, status, etc.;
3   a means to enhance sexual allure.

Exponents of the first kind of explanation list the body among other artistic forms without special attention. This tradition developed with Boas, whose work established the agenda for an anthropological analysis of body decoration. His focus, however, was less the significance and uses of body decoration than the patterns created; especially fascinating for Boas was the tendency for decoration to cover the whole bodily surface in an asymmetrical design (Boas, 1955: 32, 190–1, 217–18, 250–1). This asymmetry contrasts with the preference in western design for symmetry especially concerning the body which is generally treated as two mirror images.[5]

Boas was particularly interested in technique and significance of blurring of categories in the decorative process – between humans, animals, things and symbols – both in the formal elements of design and in the choice and use of surface. This merging of categories in representational techniques suggests a conceptual fluidity and interdependence that cannot be represented in the taxonomic principles that underpin anthropological frameworks. For Boas, masks epitomize this multiplicity of referents and registers.

Body painting consequently is predicated on the metamorphosis of one body type into another; Boas cites the example of the North American Kwakiutl Indians, one of whose designs involved painting the body all over to represent the frog, depicting the eyes and mouth of the frog on the small of the back and over the buttocks, painting frog legs down the back of the arms, and depicting the frog's back, hind legs, etc. on the front of the painted body: 'In other words, the frog is shown in such a way as though the body of the person were the frog' (ibid.: 251).

This principle of transforming the human body to be painted into other forms needs to be stressed over the usual emphasis on decorating *onto* the existing bodily form. Explanations for this belief in metamorphosis or transformative forms have been given in terms of religious, symbolic, and sociological principles but a basic difference in the way other societies *see* has perhaps been underplayed. Levi-Strauss, for example, records the following story without drawing out the generalized techniques of seeing that underpin the incorporation of new and interesting objects into existing regimes.

> After the Indians saw a European warship for the first time . . . the sailors noticed the next day that their bodies were covered with the anchor-shaped motifs; one Indian even had an officer's uniform painted in great detail all over his torso – with buttons and stripes, and the sword-belt over the coat-tails. (Levi-Strauss, 1976:245)

For these 'artists', the human body is not celebrated as the object to be decorated but is a *material for* decoration. This is alluded to by Levi-Strauss in his account of a woman representing a facial design on paper (for his records) (see Figure 2). She did not begin by drawing an outline of the face and drawing in eyes, nose, mouth, etc. as we would, but by drawing two profiles of the face, joined together, that we *read* as the outline of a face but which she intended as a split representation:

> This explains its extraordinary widths and its heart-shaped outline. The depression dividing the forehead into two halves is a part of the representation of the profiles, which merge only from the root of the nose down to the chin. (Levi-Strauss, 1969:253)

In so doing, the contours of the face (the surface area to be painted) is transferred onto the paper as space to be filled not as shadows and 'eye' perspective as in western art:

> It is clear that the artist intended to draw, not a face, but a facial painting. . . . Even the eyes, which are sketchily indicated, exist only as points of reference for starting the two great inverted spirals into whose structure they merge. The artist . . . respected its true proportions as if she had painted on a face and not on a flat surface. She painted on a sheet of paper exactly as she was accustomed to paint on a face. And because the paper *is* for her a face, she finds it impossible to *represent* a face on paper, at any rate without distortion. It was necessary either to draw the face

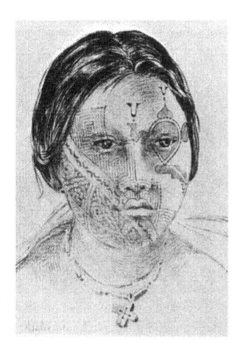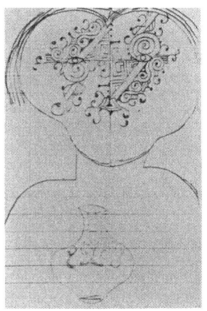

Figure 2: Contrasting spatial relationships in design
Levi-Strauss contrasts the depiction of Caduveo face-painting by an Italian artist (left) with that of a Caduveo woman (right). The bulbous shape of the head corresponds to two profiles and the flattened-out area of the face as a surface (rather like the skin of an animal) to be decorated. This produces a two-dimensional representation rather than the three-dimensional perspective of European art.

exactly and distort the design in accordance with the laws of perspective, or to respect the integrity of the design and for this reason represent the face as split in two. It cannot even be said that the artist *chose* the second solution, since the alternative never occurred to her. In native thought . . . the design *is* the face, or rather it creates it. It is the design which confers upon the face its social existence. (Levi-Strauss, 1969:258–9)

Thus whereas for Boas the technique of split representation is a representational device alluding to metamorphoses of form and symbolic connections, Levi-Strauss argues that it refers to a splitting 'between the "dumb" biological individual and the social person whom he must embody' (ibid.:259).

Decoration is actually *created* for the face, but in another sense the face is predestined to be decorated, since it is only by means of decoration that the face receives its social dignity and mystical significance. Decoration is conceived for the face, but the face itself exists only through decoration. In the final analysis, the dualism is that of the actor and his role, and the concept of *mask* gives us the key to its interpretation. (ibid.:261)

This concept of mask is not however the western one of disguising/revealing a *true identity* of the human body, but that of alluding to a split organization of actor/roles as well as of the motifs in the mask. Whereas we seek true identities that remain elusive, 'primitive' art plays on that elusiveness and illusions of 'truths' through notations that can be at least partially known and read (one could read the Paraguayan body paintings of the actors and naval uniforms in terms of this more playful quest). For Levi-Strauss, body painting functions like a snakes-and-ladders board of social contradictions and attempted resolutions, a practice he celebrates in the language of the truly noble savage:

In this charming civilisation, the female beauties trace the outlines of the collective dream with their make-up; their patterns are hieroglyphics describing an inaccessible golden age, which they extol in their ornamentation, since they have no code in which to express it, and whose mysteries they disclose as they reveal their nudity. (Levi-Strauss, 1976:256)

This passage serves as a presentiment of the third explanation of body decoration as sexual enticement – as suggested in the comment of an old missionary that tattooing among Paraguayan women made them '*more beautiful than beauty itself*' (cited by Levi-Strauss, 1969:257, my emphasis). The significance of this remark is in likening body decoration not merely to a transformative process, but as having magical or supernatural elements engaged in re-locating the image of the body in the arena of the fantastic, the land of hyperbole. For the western eyes, such excuses are closely aligned with the premise of sexual desire, and commentators resort to the use of tantalizing language to describe decorations and attribute 'motives' to their application – for example, Levi-Strauss refers to 'the almost *licentious* asymmetry of some Caduveo paintings' (ibid., my emphasis), and in a later text he asserts that:

It is fairly certain that the continuance of the custom among the women ... is to be explained by *erotic motives*. The *reputation* of Caduveo women is firmly established along both banks of the Rio Paraguay. Many half-castes and Indians belonging to other tribes have come to settle and marry at Nalike. Perhaps the facial and body paintings explain the attraction; at all events, they strengthen and symbolise it. The delicate and subtle markings, which are as sensitive as the lines of the face, and sometimes accentuate them, sometimes run counter to them, make the women delightfully *alluring*. They constitute a kind of *pictorial surgery grafting art on to the human body*. (Levi-Strauss, 1976:244, my emphasis)

Such accounts indulge in a form of pornography where the threat of sexual violence is implied and apparently tolerated, yet it appears to be constructed in the eyes and behaviour of outsiders, beholders precisely:

[Caduveo face painting] instead of representing the image of a deformed face, actually deforms a real face.... The dislocation here involves, beside the decorative value, a subtle element of *sadism*, which at least partly explains why the *erotic appeal* of Caduveo women (expressed in the paintings) formerly attracted outlaws and adventurers toward the shores of the Paraguay river. Several of these now aging men, who intermarried with the natives, described to me with *quivering emotion* the *nude bodies* of adolescent girls completely covered with interlacings and arabesques of a *perverse subtlety*. (Levi-Strauss, 1969 : 255, my emphasis)

Such lascivious thoughts were not necessarily shared by the discovered, as Szwed observes among Africans' responses to white intruders:

They were repelled by white skin, associated as it was with 'peeled' skin and leprosy, its ugly blue-veined surface shamefully covered by many clothes; these offensive-smelling Europeans with the wild-animal hair on their long heads, bodies and red faces, these savage-looking men who could live so long without their women, were seen to be cannibals. (Szwed, 1975:258)

This passage suggests that the ascription of erotica was not mutual but developed from within a particular western conceptual apparatus which roughly maps into the distinction between '*having* a body and *being* one' (Huxley, 1977:29). 'Primitive' body decoration is primarily about belonging to a collectivity despite individual variations and styles:

Within the limits of the style chosen for the occasion, big-men may mark themselves out by some eccentricity of dress, and all particpants put together their own assemblages whose details vary according to understood taste. *The final impression is one of solidarity rather than uniformity.* (M. Strathern, 1979:245, my emphasis)

The point here is that *individual* exemplification or exaggeration nonetheless contributes to the group projection, to the entire spectacle of the display. This is in stark contrast to western display which is concerned with decoration as a statement about (even *of*) individual *personality*, as captured in the saying used as the title of this article: I must put my face on. It is because of the inherent association of decoration with personality that, in fashion parades, models are frequently dressed in identical outfits, instructed to perform identical, syncopated gestures and movements, and frequently marked out as a *troupe* by the addition of some absurd headpiece or decoration that works to crush any glimpse of personality and individuality among the persons of models, and to direct attention solely towards the clothes and decorations to the invisibility of the bodies that wear them.

The Stratherns attribute this female specialization in make-up to the particularities of western sexuality, namely 'the specialisation of women as sexual objects' (A. Strathern 1981:34) and the separation of mind and body in western philosophy. Strathern suggests that this dichotomy is reflected linguistically in the distinction between 'falling in love' or 'being in love' and 'having sex': Women as sexual objects are seen as the focus of this 'animal desire', and are then dignified in terms of the ideology of love (ibid.).

Make-up not only confirms sexual attractiveness but works as an amulet with daily repetition: the cosmetic act has become a technology especially limited to the image of women as objects of male desire (ibid.:35).

The process is not simply one of enhancement but entails the construction of an ideal in which the natural face is replaced thereby 'requiring women to carry the whole "load" of artifice and sexuality' (ibid.:36). Make-up comes *to stand for* a range of social statements (Figure 3). This is the rationale behind Mary Quant's *Quant on Make-Up* which presents detailed instructions on how to achieve 'eighteen faces' which 'run the spectrum of make-up moods': 'From deceptively natural to blatantly fantastic, they are designed by top make-up artists for you to easily achieve or adapt' (Quant, 1986:n.p.).

The range of faces is designed to cover the kinds of occasions and the intended impressions that wearers literally have to 'face':

The look falls into four categories or 'occasions'; fairly natural for everyday practical wear both indoors and out; classical evening make-up for understated elegance; more expressive, light-hearted party make-up and pure fantasy for special occasions. You can, however, break the rules and cross-reference your looks to suit your own lifestyle. If you are in a profession which welcomes a more flamboyant approach to make-up, then by all means follow the lead of the more creative evening faces and adapt them to fit in with your daytime fashion philosophy. (ibid.)

The logic of this account proceeds by categorizing women's activities into types of play-acting (natural, classical, expressive, fantasy) so that even the

Figure 3: Mary Quant's faces for pleasure
The Graphic face (top) treats the face as a literal canvas for geometric design such
that the face appears as if a flat surface; the Romantic face (centre) transforms
Caduveo-type design into frivolous mystery; while the Oriental face (bottom)
combines Kabuki whitening with aggressive signs of orientalism, literally slashing
the face into asymmetrical sectors which cut through facial features.

workplace is just another scene to play out. The 'moods' of make-up pan out as impressions and effects: make-up as the art of seduction, but only ever as an allusion to, an illusion of – the face as a sexual tease. The construction of femininity as a range of teasing masks not only is the making of women but also their undoing – witness countless defences of chauvinistic behaviour, rape, and harassment on the grounds of a woman's 'provocative' dress/appearance.[6] The feminine body is a body which is treated as a canvas to be operated upon; Mary Quant's book presents the face as if it were a flat canvas upon which the 'make-up by numbers' is outlined:

It is, in a sense, a painting by numbers blueprint which graphically presents a map of the colours prior to blending . . . As make-up is itself the ultimate fashion accessory, the success of your look depends on the cross-linking of colours, textures and items in context which blend together to build the fashion impact. (Quant: n.p.)

The titles of the faces reveal a little more about women's activities:

Natural:	The No Make-up Face
	The Sporty Face
	The Quick Rescue Face
	The Stay-Put Face
Classical:	The Winter Face
	The Autumn Face
	The Spring Face
Expressive:	The Grape Face
	The Lace Face
	The Romantic Face
	The Brief Encounter Face
Fantasy:	The Flapper Face
	The Art Deco Face
	The Pop Party Face
	The Graphic Face
	The Warpaint Face
	The Oriental Face
	The Mid-Summer Madness Face

It can be noted that more faces become available towards the fantasy end of play-acting, including a seasonal deviation from the classical in mid-summer madness (as sexual deviation, perhaps?). Fantasy here entails redefining the canvas of the face totally, especially in the Graphic and Oriental Faces. The greater the fantasy, the more asymmetrical the design, suggesting the disruption of codes of design and social conventions. For example, the Oriental face constructs a threat of violence by slashing through the perceptual symmetry of the face. Of the Graphic Face, Quant writes:

The minimum of primary colours painted in bold, geometric shapes on a

Figure 4: Sonia Delaunay re-shaped the body
Delaunay's designs treated the body as geometric shapes (cones, cylinders, etc)
which were literally wrapped-up in colourful fabrics which were designed to
re-iterate those geometric shapes.

blank white canvas, produce a disarmingly abstract effect. With practice, a steady hand and an appetite for impact, your face becomes a graphic work of modern art. (ibid.: 69)

This is the radical re-casting of face and identity under the superimposition of another system of signs and cultural forms. It brings to a head the paradox that was noted by Marilyn and Andrew Strathern, since the body exhibiting the look delegates 'individuality' to the creator of other canvases. The use of art motifs (here including art deco, pop, cubism, western 'tribal', western 'oriental') has been common in the recent fashion industry.

Sonia Delaunay, for example, was one of a group of artists and designers who experimented with colour which disrupted the usual rules of colour symbolism and combinations. In conjunction with the cubist tendency 'to draw the female body in terms of simply treated, cylindrical forms' (McDowell, 1984:29), fashion design involved treating the clothes as three-dimensional canvases (cones, cylinders, capes, kimonos) to be 'painted in' as art-works (see Figure 4):

> The dynamism in her soft-edge geometric work allows both of these – form and colour, added to her response to movement and motion – to give essence and character to her concerns. . . .
>
> She was equally concerned with the spectator's relationship to her work. She felt that it had to be a transformation process, so that the spectator became more than a mere recipient, a responsive creator who could react to the notion, form and colour. (Constantine, n.d.)

Yves Saint Laurent has also borrowed from art styles but in a much more derivative way, e.g. from Mondrian, Picasso, Pop, as well as from 'exotic costume' such as Russian, Chinese, Spanish, African, etc. Yet the poaching of motifs has escaped the censure of the art world – indeed, quite the reverse – as well as the problem of copyright. Thus a scarf 'designed by' Yves St Laurent uses as its central image a Cocteau painting, yet only the (large) signature of St Laurent appears to acknowledge the feat of design!

St Laurent's derivative approach to designing, despite the flair of his creating, and his accepted position as '*the* fashion genius of the second half of the twentieth century' (McDowell: 234), relies on a highly personalized style of kinship as the fashion genre, reflected in the many eulogies that accompany his catalogues (see, for example, St Laurent, 1983). These involve the projection of the figure of St Laurent as the dictator of his customers, as an extension of himself, where eroticism is constantly implied. St Laurent's control of the gaze of fashion was consolidated with his establishment of a ready-wear line, Rive Gauche, in 1970, in order to support his haute couture (ibid.:20). This was a first for Paris. He also initiated 'designer' perfumes such as 'Y' in 1964 and 'Opium' in 1977, about which Gell observes:

> Names like 'Aphrodisia' or the elegant graphemic pun 'Y' . . . go quite far (towards implied eroticism) . . . to suggest a vast scenario of romance conducted on an epic scale. (Gell, 1977: 37)

This approach to fashion is somewhat at odds with designers like Delaunay, Vionnet, and Miyake. Vionnet's philosophy that 'you must dress a body in a fabric, not construct a dress' (McDowell: 267) evokes the approach of the Japanese designers who have challenged the parameters of Parisian design. Miyake has been especially concerned to break the rules of clothes design and fracture the ownership of bodies by designers. In particular, he has objected to the 'borrowing' of native costumes: producing no technical changes and utilized for the mere sake of appearance, they simply evoked the mode of exoticism (Isozaki, 1978:55).

The theme of exoticism is repeated in the art of make-up with Quant's manipulations of the face as canvas. The blank canvas for The Graphic Face is replaced by the creation of a mask[7] in The Oriental Face. The strength of this theatrical party look lies not only in the dramatic placing of curves and lines, which treat the face almost as if it were a mask, but in its virtually monochromatic shade scheme.

Even 'natural' faces involve forms of artifice. Thus, The Sporty Face aims to 'achieve a subtle cosmetic effect which looks deceptively natural. The idea is to enhance your face without obviously colouring it. Wear this look with casual outdoor clothes, or for sports and leisure' (Quant: 43). This subtle deception is suitable for casual occasions, but note how the look is designed to match clothes over and above occasions. The theme of deception runs right through these recipes even for The No Make-Up Face since: 'No matter how radiant or youthfully rosy your bare skin may be, lack of definition around the eyes leaves your own face "blank" and lacking vitality. Eyes need enhancing' (ibid.:49).

Femininity is thus inscribed with the techniques of painting to construct a *particular* statement of femininity – one of Quant's eighteen faces, for example. Femininity is composed of a set of roles of play-acting, all bordering on roles about sexual play (vamp, schoolgirl, film goddess, etc.). Andrew Strathern stresses the contradiction between expression of 'the self' via a 'unique' make-up/fashion style and the limited range of images of socially-recognized and accepted 'roles' which are available to women:

> The operative phrase in western culture seems to be 'I must put my face on', since 'face' refers both to an aspect of the self as individual and to the self as a stereotyped image that must be presented to others in the correct way. Insofar as 'skin' and 'face' are then considered synonymous, we arrive at the point of the mind/body dichotomy once more, since face is an aspect of the body, as opposed to the mind, in our symbol system. (A. Strathern: 36)

For Strathern, this dichotomy is gender inscribed: whereas femininity involves a subject/object dichotomy, which can never be resolved, men 'are presented as subjects, who establish their identity through their acts rather than simply through being looked at and admired. (Men) gain prestige from doing rather than being, and it is an aspect of the created "being" that cosmetics celebrate' (ibid.).

Western woman is faced with a perpetual balancing act between signifying too much femininity or signifying not enough, but her femininity is located within her make-up and gestural range, as clearly demonstrated in advertisements for chain-clothing-store fashions. The girls are dressed in fashion clothes (mini-versions of adult fashions), shaded in pastels, their hair is adorned with braids and lace, their bodies are posed in gestures of femininity, semi-balletic, semi-display, as objects of a ubiquitous gaze.[8] The boys, in contrast, are dressed in tracksuits, timeless statements of action and comfort, hair and faces unadorned, colours bright, and posed in action positions (skate-boarding). As with the latest Barbie doll, the Rockers collection, girls are constructed around passive toys and pastimes – the feature of this Barbie set is predictably the 'outrageous' rocker clothes and uniquely Barbie shape (a virtual mono-bosom, impossibly tapering torso, unnaturally shaped and extraordinarily long legs . . . and, of course, masses of very long, very thick, lustrous blond hair). Meanwhile the currently dominant boys' toys are transformers, gruesome space/monster male characters (heroes every one) who transform into high-tech space machines: the male body as action machine, and machines as an extension of the male body.

Not surprisingly, when women do active things, it is masculine gestures and forms of 'make-up' that are adopted, as reflected in business suits for women, jeans with flies, fashion tracksuits, and so on. This, however, also happens with school uniforms (see Figure 5). Here, three top designers redesign uniforms but still retain key signs of masculine (and military) clothing – blazers, ties, epaulets, 'men's' shirts, World War I-style top coats and trousers. Moreover, the illustrations of these fantasies clothe fantastic bodies, drawn with tiny heads, *huge* shoulders and torsos, and thin long legs. These blueprints bear little relation to any human bodies, let alone the variable models possessed by most schoolchildren.

Judith Okely has observed that the preoccupation with the body in school discipline and uniforms involves rules about the naked body in boys' schools as opposed to the clothed body in girls' schools: 'The presence of corporal punishment in boys' schools and its absence in girls' schools indicate differing attitudes to bodily display and contact, and possibly a differing consciousness of sexuality' (Okely, 1978 : 130).

In punishment, girls remain fully clothed and therefore their bodies remain untouchable, 'invisible, anaesthetised, and protected for one man's intrusion later' (ibid.):

As skeletons, we were corrected, ordered to sit and stand in upright lines. As female flesh and curves, we were concealed by the uniform. Take the traditional gym slip – a barrel shape with deep pleats designed to hide breasts, waist, hips and buttocks, giving freedom of movement without contour. Our appearance was neutered. (Okely : 130)

Thus, she argues, the appearance 'was neutered' by radically overriding signs of femininity through making a parody of the female body, banning

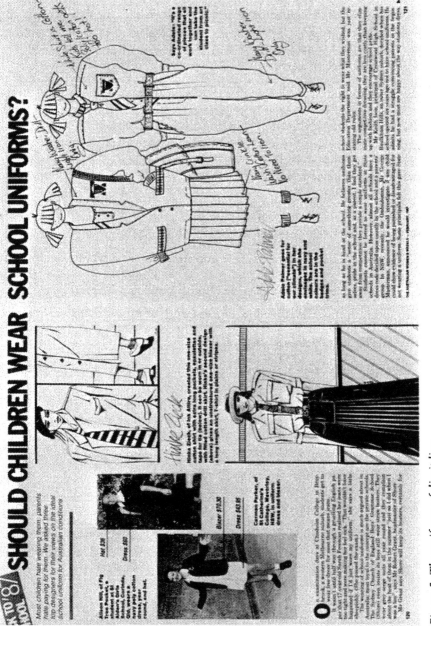

Figure 5: The uniform of discipline
The severe militarism of school uniforms features elements of traditional men's clothing – epaulets, ties, blazers, heraldry, etc. These signs are retained even in these 'designer' uniforms producing an unnecessary severity in supposedly practical clothing.

feminine clothing, and superimposing elements of masculine clothing. These features were literally inscribed onto the basic uniform:

> lace-up shoes, striped shirts, blazers, ties and tie pins. Unlike some of the boys' uniforms, ours was discontinuous with the clothes we would wear in adulthood. To us the old school tie had no significance for membership of an 'old boy network'. We were caught between a male and female image long after puberty, and denied an identity which asserted the dangerous consciousness of sexuality. Immediately we left school, we had to drop all masculine traits, since a very different appearance was required for marriageability. Sexual ripeness, if only expressed in clothes, burst out. The hated tunics and lace-ups were torn, cut, burnt or flung into the sea. Old girls would return on parade, keen to demonstrate their transformation from androgeny to womanhood. To be wearing the diamond engagement ring was the ultimate achievement. There was no link between our past and future. In such uncertainty our confidence was surely broken. (ibid. : 131)

Thus, despite the obvious signs of the female body, the basic form is continually subject to external rules of transformation, moulding and body techniques,[9] that is, femininity is the outcome of learned arrays of techniques as the *modes* and *manners* of social life. The importance of seeing femininity as a set of trainings and body techniques is that it allows the possibility of redefining that array, though this would require a disruption of the western notion of the person in terms of the category of self or ego – as 'moral power – the sacred character of the human person' (Mauss : 90), but organized by the terms of Christian morality and its gender specifications.[10]

Conclusion: peeling away to the limit

Fashion and make-up have become key players in the body techniques of femininity where the conventions of display and gesture vie with other more essential techniques,[11] in a politics of the body that transposes socio-political forms into bodily icons, where cosmetic magic is relied on over political resolution:

> We have studied the body and its 'aids' of adornment and clothing as separate media and not as a total and complete body system. . . .
> If we have failed to gain an understanding of the body as a whole system of meaning, then we have also failed to utilise the study of *corporal* form as a tool for understanding of *social* form and licence we have failed to further our understanding of social systems and social bodies. (Polhemus, 1975 : 33)

Issey Miyake's challenge to the body techniques of haute couture has been built around the philosophy of 'peeling away to the limit' initially by using irregular shaped pieces of material clinging to the body 'to take the body and clothing away from each other, reducing their relationship to the minimum' (Isozaki: 54) as a radical questioning of the very idea of (woman's) clothes:

'He smashed the image of *haute couture* as the standard bearer of fashion, as well as the idea that clothes transform those who wear them' (ibid.: 55). He has been concerned with democratizing fashion and restructuring it around the movement of bodies, and around bodies themselves:

> What he is working with is the essential space, the inconsistency between the body and the fabric. In western clothing the fabric is cut to the bodyline and sewn. The form of the attire is modelled after the body, with a shell similar to the shape of the body thus being created. In so doing, the space between the two is eliminated. In the case of japanese attire, a technique which simplifies cutting to the minimum is predominate (sic); the set width of the material itself, like an invariable constant, given importance. (ibid.: 55–6)

Miyake has combined both approaches in emphasizing the space between body and cloth by the asymmetrical draping of the cloth to give the impression of wrapping that is askew: 'in becoming conscious of peeling away, one stimulating factor was the symbolic gesture made against the methodical structure of the parisienne *haute couture*' (ibid.: 56).

The impact of his work, and of other Japanese designers, has been to re-draw the boundaries of the body for fashion away from canonical dictates and contorted 'modelling' of the clothed body towards bodies in movement and social bodies in protest, an endeavour that he has consciously allied with political movements to re-draw the techniques of the body 'confronting, shaking-up and dislocating all of the various factors that are involved in the clothing culture' (ibid.). The success of this venture is by no means guaranteed, and apparent changes can be easily relocated into new techniques and disciplines. Szwed cites the example of minstrelization which presented itself as widespread acceptance of black culture in America. In practice, it involved black entertainers engaging in a parody of body techniques which were seen to represent black culture. Thus the high-status minstrelizer has only to learn a minimal number of cultural techniques and *temporarily* mask himself as a subordinate – literally a Negro *manqué*. (Szwed: 263).

Make-up in western society produces the feminine *manqué*. Quant's faces and 'Y' perfume work as cruel parodies confining women to exotica and difference: forever unknown and unknowable.

Notes

1 The following discussion of the Hagen use of body decoration is not intended to exemplify 'the primitive' nor anthropological accounts of decoration.
2 Shortland has argued that Barthes' analysis reflects both an inability to read Japanese (literally and culturally) so that he resorts to western notions of inscrutability *as* the explanation rather than as that to be read:

> we are invited once again to contemplate (Japanese character) as enigmatic and inscrutable. The emptiness of the bodies he meets with in the Orient is a match, an explanation even, for the blankness of the face. . . . They present a

blank page without content or character, and this permits Barthes to write about them *on* them; their superficiality has, as he puts it, afforded him the situation of writing. (Shortland, 1985 : 302)

> This constitutes not an explicit resort to racism but nonetheless has the effect of 'colonizing' the Japanese body as 'the yellow hole' (ibid. : 303).

3 Cf. Edwards, 1985 : 141–7.
4 See Ennew, 1980.
5 Where asymmetry is used in western design, the fact of the disruption of that symmetry is always more significant than the overall design.
6 Cf. A. Strathern, 1981 : 36.
7 Cf. Barthes, 1973 : 56–7.
8 Cf. Frow, 1984.
9 See Mauss (1979 : 106–7) whose brief discussion of gender differences in body techniques tends to suggest a combination of physiological and sociological influences.
10 As evidenced by the ongoing dispute over the ordination of women in the Anglican church, for example.
11 Cf. Polhemus, 1975 : 32–3.

Bibliography

Angeloglou, Maggie (1970), *A History of Make-Up*, London: Studio Vista.
Anon (1987), 'Dazzling but different – the beauty secrets of Fergie and Di', *New Idea*, 14 March, pp. 12–13.
Barthes, Roland (1973), 'The face of Garbo', in *Mythologies*, St Albans: Paladin, pp. 56–7.
Barthes, Roland (1982), *Empire of Signs*, New York: Hill & Wang.
Barthes, Roland (1984), *The Fashion System* (trans. M. Ward and R. Howard), New York: Hill & Wang.
Benthall, J. and Polhemus, T. (eds) (1975), *The Body as a Medium of Expression*, London: Allen Lane.
Blacking, John (ed.) (1977), *The Anthropology of the Body*, London: Academic.
Blair, Juliet (1982), 'Private parts in public places: the case of actresses', in Shirley Ardener (ed.), *Women and Space*, London: Croom Helm.
Boas, Franz (1955), *Primitive Art*, New York: Dover.
Brain, Robert (1979), *The Decorated Body*, London: Hutchinson.
Corson, Richard (1981), *Fashions in Make-Up*, London: Peter Owen.
Craik, Jennifer (1984), 'Fashion, clothes, sexuality', *Australian Journal of Cultural Studies*, 2, 1, pp. 67–83.
Douglas, Mary (1973), *Natural Symbols*, 2nd edn, London: Barrie & Jenkins.
Edwards, Betty (1985), *Drawing on the Right Side of the Brain*, Glasgow: Fontana/Collins.
Ennew, Judith (1980), 'Against exotica', unpublished paper given to research seminar, Institute of Social Anthropology, University of Oxford.
Frow, John (1984), 'Spectatorship', *Australian Journal of Communication*, 5 and 6 (January–December), pp. 21–38.
Gell, Alfred (1975), *Metamorphosis of the Cassowaries*, London: Athlone.
Gell, Alfred (1977), 'Magic, perfume, dream . . .', in I. Lewis (ed.), *Symbols and Sentiments*, London: Academic, pp. 25–38.
Heath, Stephen (1982), *The Sexual Fix*, London: Macmillan.

Huxley, Francis (1977), 'The body and the play within the play', in John Blacking (ed.), *The Anthropology of the Body*, London: Academic, pp 29–38.
Isozaki, Arata (1978), 'What are clothes? . . . a fundamental question', in Issey Miyake, *East Meets West*, Tokyo: Heibonsha, pp. 54–6.
James, Sue (1984), *The Princess of Wales Fashion Handbook*, London: Orbis.
Keenan, Brigid (1977), *The Women We Wanted to Look Like*, London: Macmillan.
Levi-Strauss, Claude (1969), 'The art of Asia and America', in *Structural Anthropology*, London: Allen Lane.
Levi-Strauss, Claude (1976), *Tristes Tropiques*, Harmondsworth: Penguin.
Martyn, Norma (1976), *The Look. Australian Women in their Fashion*, Sydney and Melbourne: Cassell Australia.
Mauss, Marcel (1979), *Sociology and Psychology*, London: Routledge & Kegan Paul.
McDowell, Colin (1984), *McDowell's Directory of Twentieth Century Fashion*, London: Frederick Muller.
Miyake, Issey (1978), *East Meets West*, Tokyo: Heibonsha.
Munday, Jack (1986), '"I'm no natural beauty", Linda Evans reveals', *Courier-Mail*, 5 November, p. 13.
Polhemus, Ted (1975), 'Social bodies', in J. Benthall and T. Polhemus (eds), *The Body as a Medium of Expression*, London: Allen Lane, pp. 13–35.
Quant, Mary (1986), *Quant on Make-Up*. London: Century Hutchinson.
St Laurent, Yves (1983), *Yves Saint Laurent*, London: Thames & Hudson.
Shortland, Michael (1985), 'Skin deep: Barthes, Lavater and the legible body', in *Economy and Society*, 14, 3 (August), pp. 273–312.
Stern, Lesley (1982), 'The body as evidence', *Screen*, 23, 5, pp. 38–60.
Strathern, Andrew (1977), 'Why is shame on the skin?', in J. Blacking (ed.), *The Anthropology of the Body*, London: Academic, pp. 99–110.
Strathern, Andrew (1981), 'Dress, decoration, and art in New Guinea', in Malcolm Kirk (ed.), *Man as Art: New Guinea Body Decoration*, London: Thames & Hudson, pp. 15–36.
Strathern, Andrew and Marilyn (1971), *Self-Decoration in Mount Hagen*, London: Duckworth.
Strathern, Marilyn (1979), 'The self in self-decoration', *Oceania*, 48, pp. 241–57.
Szwed, John F. (1975), 'Race and the embodiment of culture', in J. Benthall and T. Polhemus (eds), *The Body as a Medium of Expression*, London: Allen Lane, pp. 253–70.
Tolmach Lakoff, Robin and Scherr, Raquel L. (1984), *Face Value. The Politics of Beauty*, London: Routledge & Kegan Paul.

Acknowledgements

Permission to reproduce material is gratefully acknowledged from the following:
Figure 1 (left). Photo by Rob Walls, 'Goroka's last picture show', *Sydney Morning Herald Good Weekend Magazine*, 11 October 1986, p. 54. Permission from Rob Walls/Rapport.
Figures 1 (right), 3 (centre), 3 (left) and 3 (right). Mary Quant, *Quant on Make-up*, Century Hutchinson Ltd, London, 1986, pp. 52, 68, 70, and 76.
Figure 2 (left and right). Claude Levi-Strauss, *Structural Anthropology*, translated by Claire Jacobson and Brooke Grundfest Schoepf, Penguin Books Ltd, 1968, copyright Basic Books Inc., 1963, plates VI and VII.

Figure 4. Sonia Delaunay, 'Costume Toupies, 1922', collection of Jacques Damase, reproduced in J. Demase et al., (eds), *Sonia Delaunay: Rhythms and Colours*, Thames & Hudson Ltd, London. Original publisher Hermann Editeurs, Paris.

Figure 5. D. Forster, 'Should children wear school uniforms?', *Australian Women's Weekly*, February 1987, pp. 120–1, Australian Consolidated Press Ltd.

ED COHEN

THE 'HYPERREAL' VS. THE 'REALLY REAL': IF EUROPEAN INTELLECTUALS STOP MAKING SENSE OF AMERICAN CULTURE CAN WE STILL DANCE?

U pon finding themselves waylaid in the 'new' world during the Second World War, the rigorously 'academized', 'disciplined', and 'philosophized' members of Frankfurt's Institute for Social Research were profoundly disoriented by American culture. Almost immediately, they recognized that the proliferating forms of commodity consumption which confronted them daily in their land of asylum confounded the post-Enlightenment meta-narratives which had made their experience 'meaningful' in pre-war Europe. Thrown from the fires of Hitler's Reich into those wartime frying pans, New York and Los Angeles, Adorno, Horkheimer, Marcuse, and their comrades viewed the 'mass culture' emanating from these two poles of US urban existence as the epitome of capitalist-produced 'rationalization' – a more developed if less sinister form of the hysterical 'rationalization' pursuing its 'final solution' in their native Germany.

Since they were surrounded by a culture whose manifestations they could all too fearfully perceive but whose 'logic' persistently eluded them, the famous German culture critics, quite understandably, fell back upon the aesthetic paradigms of their native land in order to provide themselves with a theoretical foothold on this *terra incognita*. Employing European modernism's philosophical underpinnings to comprehend the American version of capitalism's rationalizing process, they 'dialectically' contrasted the 'manipulation' of American 'mass culture' to the 'utopian' resistance which they believed to inhere in European 'Art', interpreting the former as the frightening and degenerate shadow of the latter (TABLOID, 1980). Steeped in the traditions of European 'high culture', the German ex-patriots believed that 'Art' could evoke the liberation of 'human essence'. Hence, by implicitly *and* necessarily juxtaposing the imaginative possibilities (re)presented in 'work of art' to the material limitations of (American) history, they

25

described the aesthetic experience as providing individuals with a critical – if not 'shocking' – awareness of the oppression inhering in their historical situation: 'In giving downtrodden humans a shocking awareness of their own despair the work of art professes a freedom which makes them foam at the mouth' (Horkheimer, 1982:280). Mass culture, on the other hand, could only manipulate the individual's 'real needs' leading him or her to seek 'solutions' in the frenetic pleasures proffered by commodity culture: 'What today is called popular entertainment is actually demands, evoked, manipulated and by implication deteriorated by the cultural industries (Horkheimer, 1982:288). American mass culture, as seen through the eyes of these European intelligentsia (and it was, for them, an entirely 'spectacular' approach), (re)presented only degraded, dehistoricized, or defiled 'real' human needs finding their 'false' solutions in cars, clothes, movies, magazines, etc., etc., etc.

Unfortunately, this bewildering vision of goods chasing after needs chasing after goods blurred the at times brilliant lucidity of the Frankfurt School's critical reflections on American culture. So daunted were they by the plethora of products which the 'cultural industries' disgorged that they were entirely unable to comprehend that besides 'manipulating' human needs *it is possible for individuals to find in commodities meanings that have nothing to do with their uses and functions* (TABLOID, 1980:8). For these European interpreters, the 'real' possibilities that they found in the works of 'great art' – possibilities which, indeed, defined such works – i.e., 'negation' and 'sublation', were incommensurable with the artefacts they saw in such profusion in the US. And since they believed that these cultural products must necessarily displace all 'liberatory' aesthetic potential, they implicitly juxtaposed the products of American mass culture to a 'more real' or 'more utopian' antecedant (e.g., 'art', 'reality', 'nature', etc.) without reflecting upon the historical applicability of this opposition to American (con)texts. Thus, in creating a dichotomy between the 'real' and the 'false' where the 'real' lay behind in Europe and the 'false' was omnipresent in America, the Frankfurt School provided the foundations for an ongoing Eurocentric cultural critique that consistantly fails to address the specificity of *how* the products of American mass culture are consumed or to interrogate the ways in which such consumptive patterns consolidate and/or interrupt hegemonic configurations of power in this country.

Ever since this self-limiting version of 'manipulation theory' first made its appearance in the writings of the German critical theorists, many European cultural analyses of the US have either explicitly or implicitly elaborated upon these responses to twentieth-century America's disturbing 'reality'. For example, the title essays in Umberto Eco's collection, *Travels in Hyperreality* (1986), containing the travelogue of a more recent European visitor to this land of consumer addiction, typify the pessimistic tradition of European intellectuals reflecting on the 'manipulated reality' of American life (although, admittedly, in the Reagan era there is much material to sustain such pessimistic European criticism). Originally written for the Italian press in 1975 as reflections upon his trip across the US in search of the

'Absolutely Fake' – a 'hyperreal' version of the holy grail – Eco's articles chronicle his journey through American wax museums, castles, cemeteries, museums, hotels, and amusement parks in a quest for the ultimate misrepresentation of the 'real'. On his route through New York, Florida, New Orleans, and California, the famed Italian semiotician scans the cultural landscape in search of the 'signs' which mark our signifying mania and joyfully ogles each artefact he finds. Yet underlying the results of Eco's observations, which always attempt to provide humour, provocation, and insight, lurks a latent ambivalence if not hostility towards the objects of his attention – an ambivalence that often obscures his interpretations of American culture in a cloud of European expectations.

Perhaps this underlying tension can be explained, in part, by noting that the objects most visible to this Italian *planeur* – i.e., the *flaneur* who travels exclusively by car or plane – are, not coincidentally, those objects which remind him most of home. Since he spends much of his time in the US digging up a multitude of wax, wooden, and stone copies of such high marks of European culture as the Venus de Milo, Michelangelo's David (11), Leonardo's Last Supper (7 between SF and LA), and various *pletas*, not to mention assorted bits and pieces of Greek and Roman architecture and sculpture, parts of Venetian ecclesiastical buildings, palazzos, loggia, and miscellaneous other European artefacts, it is hardly surprising that he perceives them as the cultural equivalents of fast food. These deconstructed 'originals', copies, or copies of copies, bear witness, according to the peripatetic semiotician, to the dehistoricizing effects of commodity capital-ism in the US which through the twin processes of reduplication and commodification efface all distinctions between the 'genuine' and the 'fake'. On the one hand, the 'genuine' – which Eco aligns with 'truth', 'nature', and 'reality' – exists in its cultural/natural context, thereby signifying 'history' as well as 'creativity'; on the other hand, the 'fake' – associated with 'the fantastic', 'the oneiric', and, most characteristically, 'the movies' – invokes the high-tech bricolage of 'a country with much future but no historical reminiscence'. Here, Eco implicitly reveals his diagnosis of the American cultural neurosis: our historical 'lack' – which is doubly reflected in our fixation on the future – engenders a semiotic 'desire' whose constant deferral results in an obsessive (re)presentation of a lost object ('reality', 'truth', 'nature', 'art') through the symbolic (filmic) fantasies of popular culture. (And here, of course, California and Florida, those notorious lands without a past, those fountains of eternal youth, loom large.)

Thus, as Eco reports on such illustrous spots as Disneyland and its updated sibling Disneyworld, the Hearst Castle, the Getty Museum, Ripley's Believe it or Not Wax Museum(s), the San Diego Zoo, Knotts Berry Farm, the LBJ Library, Marine World-USA, and the Madonna Inn among many others, he almost necessarily finds in them the traces of America's compulsive obsession with representation. Mediated through the con-sumptive production of a late capitalist society, this representational hysteria appears to Eco in a myriad of sometimes humorous, sometimes frightening cultural tics. However, since each stop on his itinerary always provides him with further symptoms to report and explain to the folks back home, 'believe it or not . . .', he sometimes seems overwhelmed by the incredible proliferation of kitsch spewed out as a consequence of our neurotic desire for 'the real thing' (as in 'Coke is . . .'). Yet in spite of his disorientation, Eco labours heroically on to provide some insight into the underlying representational calculus which organizes the 'freak show':

> Knowledge can only be iconic, and iconism can only be absolute. . . . For the distance between Los Angeles and New Orleans is equal to that between Rome and Khartoum, and it is the spatial, as well as the temporal, distance that drives this country to construct not only imitations of the past and of exotic lands but also imitations of itself. (p. 53)

Since Eco argues that the geographic expanse of the US (in addition to the infamous absence of the material signs of cultural history noted above) marks out the terrain of American semiosis, he finds the self-reflexive re-presentation of a legitimate past a favourite American 'past-time'. In so doing, he attributes this logic of representation to the huge geographical distances required to cover the continent – distances that have only been successfully linked in the past 100 years by incredible technologies for mass communication – and thereby suggestively links the representational practices of mass culture to the preconditions for an American conception of history.

This connection between the American geopolitical context and our modes of historical representation undoubtedly points to an important nexus of symbolic exchange that merits further examination. It is disheartening to find, therefore, that Eco's own survey seems to focus instead on simply noting the degradations of European (and especially Italian) 'ART' wrought by the barbaric culture-mongering of our *nouveau arrivé* nation. In a place – specifically LA but metynomically the entire US – where 'wealth has no history', Eco finds that Americans are fixated on 'mak[ing] posterity think how exceptional the people who lived there must have been'. The assumptions implied by this *aperçu* illustrate the limits of Eco's analysis: while he makes interesting connections among important elements of American semiosis (connecting for example, significations of 'wealth', 'history', 'nationality', and 'self'), he ultimately utilizes them only to sneer humorously at our naive vulgarity. His quest for the remnants of European 'high' culture amid the grotesques of American 'low-brow' imitations reveals nothing so much as a nostalgic passion for the lost hegemony of European cultural dominion. Thus, even though sensitive to the often glaring ironies of American consumer society, Eco can only attempt to reintegrate these contradictions into a totalizing interpretative schema that longs for the lost coherence of a now dead ('colonial') symbolic order.

Another mid-1970s European critique of American signifying practices which is perhaps more fruitful – if ultimately more frustrating and less fun – than Eco's anecdotal approach, appears in Jean Baudrillard's *Simulations* (1983). Although Baudrillard's monograph does not at first glance seem to address the specificity of American experience directly – claiming, instead, to extend a *very* Gallic epistemological enquiry into the characteristics of modern symbolic exchange begun in his earlier *L'exchange symbolique et la mort* – it is not at all coincidental that he bases his entire theoretical edifice on the cultural products of American commodity capitalism. Hence, while his theoretical ruminations profess to concern the signifying practices of all contemporary (western?) societies, his text can also be read as a commentary on 'the Procession of Simulacra' that he perceives as characterizing the 'hyperreality' of our nation.

Baudrillard begins his consideration by establishing a philosophical opposition between 'the real' and the 'hyperreal'. For him, 'the real' is aligned with meaning, origins, anteriority, metaphysics, rationality, truth, reference, objective cause; 'the hyperreal', on the other hand, is of the order of 'signs', of 'simulation', characterized by 'genetic miniaturization', 'infinite reproduction', 'operational definitions', and 'absolute manipulation'. Or, as Baudrillard (in one of his many definitions) phrases it:

> In this passage to a space [i.e., the 'hyperreal'] whose curvature is no longer that of the real, nor of truth, the age of simulation thus begins with a liquidation of all referentials – worse: by their artifical resurrection in systems of signs, a more ductile material than meaning, in that it lends itself to all systems of equivalence and all combinatory algebra. It is no longer a question of imitation, nor of reduplication, nor even of parody. It is rather a question of substituting signs of the real for the real itself, that is an operation to defer every real process by its operational double, a metastable, programmatic, perfect descriptive machine which provides all the signs of the real and short circuits all its vicissitudes. (p. 4)

The terms of this definition make Baudrillard's problematic clear: the mainstays of nineteenth-century European epistemology, the 'real itself' and its significant other, 'truth', have been killed off by the cancerous prolifer-ation of late-capitalist symbolic production, only to find their corpses 'resurrected' as 'signs' of a 'meaning' they no longer possess. In a linguistic re-enactment of *The Invasion of the Body Snatchers*, these zombie symbols, the 'signs of the real', 'substitute' themselves for 'the real itself' producing an 'operational double, a metastable, programmatic, descriptive machine'. This nightmarish scenerio, based undoubtedly on Descartes' original script, contrasts the *grands recits* (to borrow from Lyotard) which legitimated the empiricist 'realism' of the last century to the 'simulations' of contemporary 'hyperreality', in order to suggest that 'simulation' inaugurates a new mode of signification.

Not surprisingly, then, Baudrillard's definitional examples of simulation are drawn from the discursive practices of some of nineteenth-century capitalism's most powerful and ubiquitous institutions: medicine, the army, religion, and ethnology (which he uses as a representative of 'science'). Drawing from the literature of nineteenth-century psychiatry (Littre), Baudrillard distinguishes between 'dissimulation' or 'feigning', and 'simu-lation', claiming that the latter disturbs the representational order which asserts the 'unreality' of the former: 'feigning or dissimulating leaves the reality principle intact: the difference is always clear, it is only masked; whereas simulation threatens the difference between "true" and "false", between "real" and "imaginary"' (p. 5). Baudrillard claims that 'simulation' is threatening to institutional discourses because it disturbs those 'truth principles' which legitimate them. For example, he finds the 'simulator' who enacts the symptoms of physiological, psychological, or sexual 'perversion' – and who is, therefore, 'equivalent to a "real" homosexual, heart-case, or lunatic' – threatening to the army because the simulator who embodies his or her 'simulation' threatens to subvert the 'classical reason' which defines these categories as absolute ('natural') signs of difference. 'Simulation is infinitely more dangerous . . . [than 'dissimulation' or 'feigning'] since it always suggests, over and above its object, that *law and order themselves might really be nothing more than a simulation*'. This threat does not arise, however, because simulation *interrupts* – i.e., directly engages and functionally displaces – the order of representation (the 'reality principle') but rather because 'the spectre raised by simulation' points out that 'truth, reference, and objective causes [which underlie nineteenth-century 'realism'] have ceased to exist.'

Although he seems quite aware that 'realism' is a social/historical product, Baudrillard unfortunately does not focus on the historical conditions which gave rise to these discursive formulations of 'the real'. Instead, resorting to the overworked case of religion, he chooses to engage in a metaphysical digression on the ontological status of language after the 'death of God'. Here, in the opposition he constructs between 'the iconoclasts' and 'the iconolaters', he locates the 'death of the real'. In Baudrillard's narrative, the iconoclasts, while seeking to preserve 'the pure and intelligible Idea of God' from the 'visible machinery of icons', ironically affirmed the power of the image over 'the Idea' by finding it worthy of attack. The iconolaters, on the other hand, 'were the most modern and adventurous minds, since underneath the idea of the apparition of God in the mirror of images, they already enacted his death and his disappearance in the epiphany of his representations.' (Baudrillard implicitly returns to this parable later in distinguishing the political demarkations between 'the left' and 'the right', finding in the attacks of the former a confirmation of the interests of the latter.) This subsumption of the 'idea of the apparition of God' beneath the 'mirror of images' provides Baudrillard with the paradigm for the death of the 'real':

Thus perhaps at stake has always been the murderous capacity of images, murderers of the real, murderers of their own model as the Byzantine icons could murder their divine identity. To this murderous capacity is opposed the dialectical capacity of representation as a visible and intelligent mediation of the Real. All of Western faith and good faith was engaged in this wager on representation: that a sign could refer to the depth of meaning, that a sign could *exchange* for meaning and that something could guarantee this exchange – God, of course. But what if God himself can be simulated, that is to say, reduced to the signs which attest his existence? Then the whole system becomes weightless, it is no longer anything but a gigantic simulacrum – not unreal, but a simulacrum, never again exchanging for what is real, but exchanging in itself, in an uninterrupted circuit without reference or circumference. (pp. 10–11)

In this dehistoricized fable recounting the 'murder' of divine 'authority', Baudrillard seeks to illustrate the conditions which predicate the representational order of the 'hyperreal'. The 'murderous capacity of images' overwhelms 'the dialectical capacity of representation as a visible and intelligible mediation of the Real', thereby abandoning the very possibility for 'realistic' representation to contemporary culture's rapacious hunger for raw signifying material.

Hence, according to Baudrillard, to analyse contemporary culture in terms of a (Marxist) notion of 'ideology', which conversely posits the possibility for a 'scientific' vantage point on the real, demonstrates an atavistic attempt to return to a 'theology of truth and secrecy' denied to this 'age of simulacra and simulation'. Instead, Baudrillard offers the notion of 'nostalgia' to explain the contemporary mode of symbolization: 'When the real is no longer what it used to be, nostalgia assumes its full meaning. There is a proliferation of myths of origin and signs of reality; of second-hand truth, objectivity, and authenticity.' Nostalgia – itself, not coincidentally, often deemed a specific form of 'ideology' – functions by resurrecting the corpses of earlier 'realities' and deploying them to attest to the continued life of 'the real'. Myths of origin substantiate this resurrection by seeming to confirm a teleological progression from the past to the present, that is, by confirming history as having meaning for us now. For Baudrillard, this 'order of history' is illusory because the 'reality' to which it refers has been occluded by the same signs which make it 'meaningful'; therefore, he substitutes for the language of 'history' the language of film which he sets forth as the icon of the insubstantial: 'We too live in a universe everywhere strangely familiar to the original – here things are duplicated by their own scenario.' Of course, the irony of Baudrillard's substitution here lies in the surreptitious re-entry of the 'original' as the model that the 'scenario' copies. Since it lurks beneath the phantom filmic 'hyperreal', it is ultimately the 'real' (through its implicit plenitude) that guarantees the ghostly 'duplications' of simulation. Thus, as Baudrillard mimes (mines?) a metaphysics of presence in order to suggest – like the shadows in Plato's cave – the illusory quality of its 'reality', his own shadow reappears stalking him silently, but persistently, from behind.

After attempting to deconstruct the nexus of history and representation, Baudrillard (like Eco) turns to an analysis of American popular culture to confirm his insights; the first example being, of course, Disneyland. Like the good European critic that he is, Baudrillard finds in Disneyland the proof that LA – but as with Eco, also metynomically the entire US – is 'nothing more than an immense script and a perpetual motion picture':

Disneyland is there to conceal the fact that it is the 'real' country, all of 'real' America, which *is* Disneyland (just as prisons are there to conceal the fact that it is the social that is entirely carceral). Disneyland is presented as imaginary in order to make us believe that the rest is real, when in fact all of Los Angeles and the America surrounding it are no longer real, but of the order of the hyperreal and simulation. (p. 25)

For Baudrillard, Disneyland is a simulation of the 'imaginary' which seems to confirm the existence of a 'reality' somewhere else. This 'nostalgia' for an order of representation that is now 'dead' reanimates the mechanical figures that inhabit the amusement park, investing them with a facsimile of life which suggests that the living are elsewhere. From this play of reduplication and 'animation' Baudrillard concludes that 'it is no longer a question of a false representation of reality (ideology) but of concealing the fact [???] that the real is no longer real, and thus of saving the reality principle'. (With this dismissal of the possibility for an 'ideological' critique, Baudrillard indicates that beneath his analysis of 'nostalgia' as the tactical preservation of the 'reality principle' lies an attack on the marxist and neo-marxist narratives of commodity capitalism – an attack which accelerates through the rest of the text.)

Similarly, Baudrillard analyses Watergate as a simulation of a political scandal, which by invoking the signs of a moral transgression affirms the continued viability of a verifiable moral code:

all those scenarios of deterrence, like Watergate, try to regenerate a moribund principle by simulated scandal, phantasm, murder – a sort of hormonal treatment by negativity and crisis. It is always a question of proving the real by the imaginary, proving truth by scandal, proving law by transgression, proving the work by strike, proving the system by crisis and capital by revolution.

Baudrillard's analysis of Watergate as the model for the 'crisis mentality', that has since characterized the relationship between the American media and the state, undoubtedly points to a very present condition of political legitimation in the US. The executive branch of the American government, especially as enacted by 'the Great Communicator', Ronald Reagan, has come to rely increasingly on television reporting of 'the crisis of the week' as testimony to the 'effectivity' of presidential authority. Hence, Baudrillard's suggestion – even before Ronnie Raygun – that 'they [American presidents] nevertheless needed that aura of an artificial menace to conceal that they were nothing other than mannequins of power', points to a now ubiquitous strategy of Presidential (re)action. Simultaneously asserting the immediacy and necessity of wide-ranging executive powers, the 'simulation' of presidential 'strength' – a familiar Reagan credo – reasserts the legitimacy of the underlying models that make such displays of power possible.

However, Baudrillard's concomittant claim that this particular 'strategy of the Real' constitutes a condition of 'the political' and thereby delimits a new order of signification aimed at 'reinject[ing] realness and referentiality everywhere, in order to convince us of the reality of the social, of the gravity of the economy and the finalities of production', overstates the uniqueness of this epistemological undertaking. In fact, to a large extent, Baudrillard's analysis, rather than pointing to a new order of symbolic exchange, seems instead to provide a timely update of Marx's *tour de force* assessment – in *The Eighteenth Brumaire* – of the technologies employed by the bourgeois state in its ('ideological'?) self-legitimation. For, whereas Marx only demonstrates the manner in which nineteenth-century ideology cloaked itself in the narratives of the past in order to legitimate the 'crises' of its present, Baudrillard – even though he repudiates 'ideology' as predicated on a now dead 'real' – demonstrates quite perceptively the array of representational modes and practices through which contemporary political power puts on the clothing of the past in order to carry out its projects in the present.

To Baudrillard, however, this historical construction delimits not just a strategy but a 'logic' which derives from (surprise!) the workings of 'capital'.

> Hyperreality and simulation are deterrents of every principle and of every objective; they turn against power this deterrance which it so well utilized for a long time against itself. For, finally, it was capital which was the first to feed throughout its history on the destruction of every referential, of every ideal distinction between true and false, good and evil, in order to establish a radical law of equivalence and exchange, the iron law of power. It was the first to practice deterrance, abstraction, disconnection, deterritorialization, etc.; and if it was capital which fostered reality, the reality principle, it was also the first to liquidate it in the extermination of every use value, of every real equivalence, of production and wealth, in the very sensation we have of the unreality of the stakes and the omnipotence of manipulation. Now it is this very logic which is hardened even more *against* it. And when it wants to fight this catastrophic spiral by secreting one last glimmer of reality, on which to found one last glimmer of power, it only multiplies the *signs* and accelerates the play of simulation.
> (pp. 43–4)

In Baudrillard's analysis, the crushing blows which capitalism rained down upon the primary oppositions of classical representation ('true'/'false', 'good'/'evil') in the propagation of its own 'radical law of equivalence and exchange' have pitilessly returned – like the Angel of Death – to slay its first-born. However, the 'power' which instigated the signifying 'logic' of capitalist exchange is also dying with its offspring. As if to stave off the inevitable, Baudrillard suggests, power doubles back upon itself and 'risks the real, risks crisis, it gambles on remanufacturing artificial, social, economic, political stakes'. Here, Baudrillard seems almost prescient, characterizing *avant-propos* the official response to the latest White House escapades that have spawned a series of media-enhanced Watergate simulacra: 'Irangate', 'Contragate', 'Cocaine-gate', 'CIA-gate', etc. The 'powers that be' caught in their own web of dissimulation are the necessary sacrifices that will (hopefully) appease the angry god who threatens to bring them down and thereby re-establish the order that enables them to continue to play the game which has brought them down. The sight of Ed Meese declaring that 'the President wants the entire truth' is strong proof of Baudrillard's contention: executive power certainly seems to gamble dangerously these days. Yet even while the current political situation would seem to warrant Baudrillard's analysis, it still demands a heady leap to jump from the specificity of particular styles of political signification to a declaration of the 'characteristic hysteria of our time'.

In undertaking to globalize his perceptions – and perhaps in this way to 'simulate' a historical analysis – Baudrillard places himself in clear opposition to those who would define the knowledge-effects of power as 'ideology':

> it is no longer a question of the ideology of power, but of the *scenario* of power. Ideology only corresponds to a betrayal of reality by signs; simulation corresponds to a short-circuit of reality and to its reduplication by signs. It is always the aim of ideological analysis to restore the objective process; it is always a false problem to want to restore the truth beneath the simulacrum. (p. 48)

Baudrillard's substitution of the language of cinema ('scenario') for the language of 'truth' ('ideology') is designed to evoke the transformations of signification endemic to media-saturated western societies. He appeals to the apparently self-evident 'fantasy' of movies as proof of the 'short-circuit of reality and . . . its reduplication by signs'. Yet this substitution is itself conditioned by the historical emergence of film (and metonymically all mass media) as a specific signifying apparatus within the context of twentieth-century advanced capitalism and, as recent film theory has shown, this apparatus must be considered as both produced by and productive of concrete technologies of signification. Thus, when Baudrillard rhetorically embraces the metaphors of film as defining the contours of simulation, he does so only by ignoring the complicating factor that cinema is not *sui generis* but rather an overdetermined nexus of meaning production.

This abstraction from the concrete particulars of filmic semiosis to a larger order of symbolic exchange becomes readily apparent in the example Baudrillard employs to confirm ideology's moribund stature. Citing the now infamous PBS series, 'An American Family', Baudrillard contends that the television rendering of the Loud family's implosion characterizes a new non-relation to the 'real': 'Here the real can be seen to have never existed (but "as if you were there"), without the distance which produces perspective space and our depth vision (but "more true than nature")'. By literalizing the perspectival space which imbues post-Renaissance representations of 'the real', Baudrillard suggests that television undermines the mechanisms upon which it predicates its own signification, demonstrating the illusory nature of its own production even as it continues to reassert the 'reality' of this illusion. In so doing, it reiterates the vacuousness of its 'reality-effect' and thereby becomes an icon of simulation, the virtual DNA of the 'hyper-real':

we must think of the media as if they were, in outer orbit, a sort of genetic code which controls the mutation of the real into the hyper-real. . . . The whole traditional mode of causality is brought into question: the perspective, deterministic mode, the 'active', critical mode, the analytical mode – the distinction between cause and effect, between active and passive, between subject and object, between ends and means. It is in this mode that it can be said: TV watches us, TV alienates us, TV manipulates us, TV informs us. (p. 55)

That Baudrillard returns to McLuhan's classic formulation to epitomize the 'hyperreal' illustrates the degree to which his characterization of the elision of cause and effect, active and passive, subject and object, ends and means is predicated on an earlier, surreptitious, elision of 'medium' and 'message'. In other words, Baudrillard's formulation of 'simulation' over and against 'ideology' is dependent on the breakdown of the latter's immunity to the infectious non-differentiation 'communicated' via the media: 'Everywhere, in whatever political, biological, psychological, media domain, where the distinction between poles can no longer be maintained, one enters into simulation, and hence into absolute manipulation.'

For Baudrillard, then, as for Horkheimer and Adorno before him, mass media have become the medium of 'manipulation' *par excellence*. Yet by presupposing mass media's 'manipulation' as the limit point of contemporary symbolic exchange, he necessarily occludes a consideration of the specific strategies whereby these media (re)produce knowledge-effects in concrete historical (con)texts. It is as if, by assuming the fatality of the media's infectious powers, Baudrillard has abandoned 'the real' while the corpse is still breathing so that he himself can transcend the realm of vulnerability. Indeed, in a recent interview with Sylvere Lotringer, Baudrillard remarks: 'Theory itself is simulation. At least, that's how I use it' (1986). Here Baudrillard seems to embrace simulation in order to affirm the impossibility of an encounter with the real; as he says in the same interview, history is now for him 'an immense toy'. Unfortunately for those of us who have not yet come to terms with this unwieldy plaything, it may still be more useful to continue to try to conjecture how to handle it safely without harming either ourselves or each other. Thus, while Baudrillard's acute perceptions on the strategies of 'simulation' throw new light upon the interplay of meaning and power in our media age, they do not yet obviate the need for a clearer formulation of the 'rules of the game'.

It is precisely for this reason that it is necessary for American students of mass culture to reject the distance which European culture critics have maintained in relation to their objects of study and to engage the artefacts of commodity culture as elements of our own historical experience. In so doing, we will be able to confront the difficult contradictions which these commodities raise both at the level of theory and perhaps, more problematically, at the level of practice. As Tania Modleski points out in the introduction to her excellent new collection of cultural criticism, *Studies in*

Entertainment (1986):

> Unlike the members of the Frankfurt School, who came from another
> country with its very different traditions and found themselves relocated
> in an alien culture, the new generation [of culture critics] is composed of
> people who grew up on mass culture – literally danced to the kind of
> 'standardized' music which so alarmed Theodor Adorno that he pondered
> how to turn jitterbugging 'insects' back into men and women. (p. x)

The importance of approaching mass culture from the dance floor and not
just from an armchair or a desk should not be underestimated. Since mass
culture is by definition shared by large numbers of individuals, it demands a
critical perspective which both respects and analyses the diversity of
practices which constitute it. This attitude of engagement, then, will permit
us to begin to construct new approaches to 'mass culture' that neither
abstract nor oversimplify our objects of study, and thereby to embark on a
serious *and* 'entertaining' reappraisal of this complex phenomenon now
seemingly endemic to western capitalist societies.

While the best of contemporary culture studies call upon widely varied
theoretical strategies to develop their insights, they are relatively unified in
seeking out the areas of uncertainty and ambiguity in the 'mass' phenomena
that they address in order to examine the strategies through which particular
texts, artefacts, and experiences both articulate and inflect a range of social
and historical relations. This undertaking sets them apart from earlier
'manipulation theories' in that it obviates the need to implicitly juxtapose
the products of mass culture to a 'more real', 'more authentic', or 'more
utopian' antecedant (e.g., 'art', 'reality', 'nature', etc.) and thereby allows
the reconsideration of the cultural bases that underlies this very distinction.
As one recent *culturateur* remarks:

> Rather than understanding formal innovation to be a deconstruction of
> dominant ideology, we might want to deconstruct the whole underlying
> philosophy of a critical practice that places innovation and dominance in
> opposition, that understands mass culture to be an ideological form that is
> most effective when it is formally and thematically most simple. I would
> suggest that much of our contemporary critical theory has been blocked in
> its analysis of cultural politics today by its reliance on a belief in the stable
> existence of a whole series of reductive dichotomies; on the univocal
> valorization of one term in the dichotomy over the other; and on the
> assumption that a number of different dichotomies are parallel, equiv-
> alent, or even interchangeable (as in the process by which an opposition of
> 'simple' and 'complex' is mapped onto oppositions of 'mass culture' and
> 'high culture' or, in recent work, onto oppositions of 'hegemonic' (or
> ideological) and 'counterhegemonic' (or subversive). (Polan, 1986: 170)

This characterization acutely describes the implicit importation of the
oppositions generated by European 'modernist' aesthetics into the methodologies employed throughout most twentieth-century cultural analysis. When
the 'utopian' or 'liberatory' moments of cultural experience are predicated

upon a previous valorization of 'innovation' as the 'negation' or 'transgression' of 'dominance', the effective analysis of those artefacts which (re)produce this 'dominance' is necessarily circumvented. Since they are clearly neither 'negative' nor 'transgressive', the products of mass culture are always already seen in these types of theoretical undertakings as 'ideological' – usually aligned here with 'false consciousness' – thereby effacing the very process which needs explanation, i.e., *how* the products of mass culture participate in the (re)production of cultural and economic hegemony. Thus, it is only by reconciling the legacy of the Frankfurt School and of those other European critics who have since followed them across the Atlantic with the historical particularities of American mass culture that we will be able to begin to understand how we dance on our own two feet.

References

Baudrillard, Jean (1983), *Simulations*, trans. Paul Foss, Paul Patton, Phillip Beitchman, New York: Semiotext.

Eco, Umberto (1986), *Travels in Hyperreality*, New York: Harcourt, Brace, Jovanovitch.

Horkheimer, Max (1982), 'Art and mass culture', in M. O'Connell (trans.), *Critical Theory*, New York: Continuum.

Lotringer, Sylvere (1986), 'Forgetting Baudrillard', *Social Text*, 5 : 3.

Modleski, Tania (1986) (ed.), *Studies in Entertainment: Critical Approaches to Mass Culture*, Bloomington: Indiana University Press.

Polan, Dana (1986), 'Brief encounters: mass culture and the evacuation of sense', in T. Modleski, *Studies in Entertainment*.

TABLOID COLLECTIVE (1980), 'On/against mass culture theories', *Tabloid: A Review of Mass Culture and Everyday Life*', 1–2 (Spring–Summer).

JON STRATTON

DECONSTRUCTING THE TERRITORY

' **A** ustralian' history has traditionally located itself in a factual history of white settlement occurring from the south-east of the continent. The north of the continent has been constructed as the site of the Other, of that which has been repressed in the south's production of the real. The area denoted as the Northern Territory is the least 'real' area of Australia, and is, therefore, the weakest moment in the articulation of the dominant discourse of 'Australia'.

National history is one inflection of the discourse of nationality. Traditionally, such history seeks to construct the idiosyncracy of the nation it tautologically helps to produce by identifying empirical, material matters of special uniqueness to that nation. In Australia such a historiography can be partly traced in the lineage of Keith Hancock's *Australia* (1930) to Russel Ward's *The Australian Legend* (1958) and, perhaps most classically, Manning Clark's voluminous *A History of Australia* (1962–). Clark's work, in particular, is distinguished by his attempt to locate the specificity of Australia in a range of particular empirical occurrences; the discourse constructed from within by the force of its own material effectivity. White, in his book on Australian identity, *Inventing Australia*, has cast a shadow over this faith in the empirical. He writes:

> So we will never arrive at the 'real' Australia. From the attempts of others to get there, we can learn much about the travellers and the journey itself, but nothing about the destination. There is none. (White, 1981:x)

The real Australia, then, is a chimera, an appearance generated by the force of, let us say, desire. The real Australia is a determining absence at the centre of national historical discourse, the Other which generates the system. In this article I will argue that within the constitution of the discourse of Australia the Northern Territory, and Darwin in particular, occupy the moment of closure of the system. The discourse of Australia constructs reality through the assumptions of positivist empiricism. Australia defines itself discursively in relation to the Northern Territory which is signalled in a variety of ways which will be discussed below as less real.

Geographically, the system of Australia (appears to) constitute(s) itself from the urban south. The empirical history of Australia constructs itself from Sydney and Melbourne. The further north one goes the less historically meaningful geographical Australia becomes. In this mythic geography Western Australia and South Australia become annexes of the New South Wales/Victoria, Sydney/Melbourne axis. Queensland is a place of diminished reality and, consequently, a site of wonders. It is known in the discourse of Australia as in empirical Australian history which is part of that discourse, for its 'idiosyncracies': the first Labour government in the world, the gerrymander, police corruption, the Gold Coast, Sir Johannes Bjelke-Petersen.

In Australia, where the image of Nature has tended to be dominated by negative connotations, Sydney and Melbourne have been produced as the urban sites of civilization. In relation to these Brisbane has been constructed in the discourse as the largest country town in the world. It is, therefore, articulated as fundamentally provincial, and therefore also less real, dependent on Sydney and Melbourne in a way that Adelaide and Perth are not. In urban, industrial, capitalist society the general site of the empirical claim to reality is work. Queensland, being less real than New South Wales and Victoria, has been articulated as the touristic site of pleasure. Sydney and Melbourne may not be able to take Brisbane seriously but, precisely because of this, they will take their holidays on the Gold Coast. On the geographical journey to the limits of the discourse of Australia Queensland marks the half-way house, the moment of a difference which can be acknowledged and incorporated into the system. The moment of pleasure, the acceptable *jouissance* (the *plaisir* which comes on like *jouissance*) of the Gold Coast, marks that capacity. The discourse of Australia is not static, gradually Queensland is being realized. Tourism, as a discursive practice, is one moment in the process of realization, the moment when the repressed is still apparent as fantasy but has been made safe. Even in Queensland, however, there is the Deep North and, beyond Queensland, there is the Far North, areas which are only now undergoing the touristic process.

We need to note that, in this mythic geography, there is no Deep South or Far South; Tasmania, albeit to the resentment of Tasmanians, is constructed as an appendage of Victoria. The north, as a discursive element, exists not in relation to the south but in relation to the claimed reality of Sydney/Melbourne. The empirical facticity of cities is contrasted with a geographically constructed region. The north as a term signals itself as the site of the repressed. It is repression which gives reality to the south. There is another geographic term which complements and overlaps with the term Far North and that is the Top End. This term has been given a meteorological definition; it is the area within which the Australian tropical climate defined in terms of Wet/Dry occurs. The Top End thus has become a technical term for an area which is experientially defined as tropical. There will be much more to say on the importance of the tropics in the discourse of Australia below; here it is sufficient to point out that, as with Far North, there is no Bottom End of Australia. Discursively, the claim of heat is one important signal of the tropics. In non-tropical Australia the climate is constructed as fundamentally homogeneous in spite of large temperature variations.

The rhetoric of the Northern Territory as a frontier, as in the title of C.L.A. Abbott's *Australia's Frontier Province* (1950), signals its position as both a part of and 'beyond' the real Australia. The rhetoric of the frontier marks the moment of fracture and of repression, the limit of the national discourse's ability to represent itself. In Abbott's title the use of the term 'province' connotes the ambiguity of a colonial status. Such rhetoric of geographical and discursive limits is very powerful when Australia as a discursive whole, the nation, constitutes itself externally in relation to the Otherness of 'Asia'. In Australia's discourse Asia begins where Australia's north ends. The openness of the term 'north', its construction in terms of both internal and external definitions, leads Australia into Asia. What countries constitute Asia and where this Asia, which no longer carries its usage as a description of a continent, ends is inevitably vague. Asia is the demarcation, the limit of Australia signalled from the outside. It is from this Othering of the geographic and discursive space beyond the unreality of the north, that the sense of threat is deployed in titles such as J. Macdonald Holmes' *Australia's Open North* (1963). If the north is a frontier, and it is open then Australia's discourse is not secure. This, indeed, is one effect of the lack of realization of the north. The discourse is unstable and the Other may enter. If this occurs Australia will lose its definition.

One manifestation of the lack of empirical reality of the Northern Territory is its absence from empirical histories of Australia. In such national histories the Northern Territory is literally written out. History constructs itself from within, valorizing its subject in giving it presence, reality, through a recitation of empirical facts. In Hancock's study, *Australia*, the Northern Territory gets about two pages of discussion and one page devoted to a map of a possible rail line from Darwin to Sydney by way of Queensland.[1] The section begins with the sentence, 'Between the borders of Queensland and Western Australia lies the old Northern Territory.' (Hancock, 1966:156) Hancock is discussing tropical Australia, a very special space in Australia's discourse. He has already discussed tropical Queensland and tropical Western Australia. The Northern Territory appears as an afterthought as if it is what keeps tropical Queensland and tropical Western Australia apart. Even though some of the Northern Territory is geographically below the Tropic of Capricorn, Hancock places his discussion of the Territory within a section entitled 'Economic Geography: The Tropics'. Hancock sums up the Territory's history by quoting Sir George Buchanan:

> Sir George Buchanan, who at the invitation of the Commonwealth Government reported on the Territory in 1925, thus summed up its history: 'The Northern Territory is suffering from isolation, an inefficient system of administration, lack of communications, and constant labour troubles.' (Hancock, 1966:156)

Hancock then tells us in one sentence the administrative history of the Northern Territory. The gap between geography and history, space and time, is in modern western discourse the site of desire. Hancock demonstrates well how, in the Northern Territory, history and geography meet at the limit of Australia's discourse, the site of the repressed.

Hancock goes on to discuss the problems of the pastoral industry in the Territory, in particular the problem of peopling it. Hancock's main recommendation is the building of a railway. A railway from Darwin to the south of the country is one of the most important *topoi* in the discursive construction of the Northern Territory. Railways connect. If they connect they draw what they connect into the same system. The important *topos* of isolation in Australia's discourse is often invoked in relation to the Northern Territory. The railway is claimed as a means of making the Territory less isolated. In Australia's discourse railways are a powerful figure of integration. Western Australia is connected to the east by a railway the building of which was an important factor in Western Australia joining the Federation. In the rhetorical construction of the Northern Territory's discourse the lack of a railway, the failure to build a railway, and, of course, the abiding concern with building one signals the difference, the unreality of the Northern Territory.

A. G. L. Shaw's *The Story of Australia* acknowledges in its preface its debt to Hancock's book. It was published in 1954, some twenty-four years after Hancock's book, and Pascoe's historiography of Australian histories describes it as an example of syncretic organicism (Pascoe, 1979:93 and ch. 4): a form of Australian national history organized around themes. Not least among Shaw's themes, and one common to much Australian history, is a reworking of the Enlightenment idea of progress. This reworking employs such themes as economic development, the increase in national population, and, most importantly for the argument here, the idea of a geographical expansion from the south-east into the 'rest' of what has become Australia. This physical expansion is mobilized as a trope for the historical *topos* of continuity and acts as a legitimation for the empirical reality of what is within the frontier of the geographical expansion. This trope has operated as a strategy for emphasizing the history of white settlement over Aboriginal history. It works to give greater legitimacy, greater historical worth, to those areas first settled by whites. Such areas have a longer history, which is claimed to be constituted of more empirical facts. Conversely, more recently settled areas have less empirical facts, less history, and are therefore less real.

The effect of this formulation in Shaw's book is that out of the five references to the Northern Territory in the index only one refers to an empirical event integral to the Northern Territory (the Vestey's Meatworks project) whilst all the other references are simply strategies of inclusion. Empirical events occurring within the Northern Territory are meaningful because of their relevance to the rest of Australia. This includes the discovery of uranium in the Northern Territory where this event is not described in its own right but in relation to the problem of 'Australia's' balance of payments. Shaw writes:

> Soon after the war, uranium was opportunely discovered at Rum Jungle in the Northern Territory, alongside a railway and the major north-south

continental road, and provided valuable immediate wealth, as the government was able to negotiate an excellent long-term sales contract. (Shaw, 1972:280)

In the word 'opportunely' Shaw elides the entire history of mining in the Northern Territory. Elsewhere the Northern Territory is mentioned in association with Queensland and Western Australia (a rhetorical peripheral triumvirate which we have already found in Hancock) in the context of the treatment of Aborigines.

The first mention of the Northern Territory in Shaw's book signals its place in Australia's discourse. Shaw is discussing one of Sturt's explorations. He writes:

In July they were able to move on and found Strezlecki's Creek and Cooper's Creek, and then, farther west, Sturt's Stony Desert. Just south of the tropic, near the present border between Queensland and Northern Territory, they had to turn back. (Shaw, 1972:71)

The exploration *topos* signals the expansion of 'Australia'. The tropics – as we shall see – is one signal of the alien, the limit of the Australian real. The marker Shaw uses, the Queensland/Northern Territory border, is associated with another limit, the limit of Sturt's northern exploration. The north remains unexplored.

The one time Shaw does discuss the Northern Territory in its own right, in relation to his theme of the development of Australia as an integrated nation, the section begins like this:

Even the Northern Territory was not entirely forgotten when the Commonwealth Government took over its administration in 1911. A commission of inquiry recommended railway building to help the stock raising for which the territory is best suited. (Shaw, 1972:16)

Shaw's use of 'even', here, suggests the extreme marginalization of the Northern Territory. But its usage is more complex than this. What it does is link the narrative and conceptual structure of Shaw's book with the general discourse of Australia through a narrational attempt to invoke the complicity of the reader in the marginalization of the Northern Territory in Australia's discourse. The following sentence once again introduces the *topos* of the railway which was never built. Once more the difference of the Northern Territory is affirmed within the system of Australia.

This difference, this construction of the Northern Territory as outside the homogeneous reality of Australia, is demonstrated most clearly in its absence from historical discussion. In Manning Clark's *A Short History of Australia*, for example, first published in 1964, neither the Northern Territory nor Darwin are mentioned in the index at all. In the text, however, there is a one-sentence reference to the bombing of Darwin and Broome in 1942.[2] In Clark, as in all empiricist histories of Australia, the Northern Territory is excluded from Australian history, excluded from reality. Even Richard White's book, *Inventing Australia*, which is a book about the history of mythic constructions of Australia, excludes the Northern Territory.

Now an alternative local history is developing which attempts to integrate the Northern Territory into Australia's historical discourse by producing it as having an empirical history and therefore as being real. Ross Fitzgerald has used the same strategy for Queensland in his two-volume *A History of Queensland* (1982 and 1984). Such an empirical approach is the basis for Powell's critical description, in *Far Country*, of Ernestine Hill's *The Territory* (1951) as 'wild romanticism, literature masquerading as history, compelling singing of a great far country' (Powell, 1982:242). Local histories provide a point of connection, an opportunity to expand the history of Australia which, nevertheless, remains a history written from the south as the very title of Powell's book, *Far Country*, accepts. Powell's book attempts to write the Northern Territory into Australian history rather than the grander task of attempting to reconstruct that history. This is easily illustrated by asking what a history of 'Australia' written from a Northern – or a Northern Territorian – perspective would look like.

Histories of the Territory from Hill's *The Territory*, first published in 1951, have tended to accept the articulation of the Territory as unreal and have produced mythic histories. Powell, however, working within the empiricist framework, had to write a history against the discursive construction of the Northern Territory. He writes that:

> During the second half of this century writers, journalists and the tourist trade have promoted the image of the Territory as Australia's last frontier. But to many Australians who live south of the Tropic of Capricorn the far north is still outside the real Australia. Even the frontier image, justified in the wide sweep of the land, is plainly ridiculous when applied to Darwin. (Powell, 1982:241)

Powell, here, recognizes and critiques the dominant discursive construction of the Northern Territory. He uses the *topoi* of the far north and the tropics. Their point now, however, is to emphasise what has appeared different as being really the same. Darwin, Powell wants to argue, and by analogy the Northern Territory, is just like the rest of Australia; Darwin is just another city. Powell's empirical history is 'proof' of the reality of the Northern Territory. Having presented his empirical history Powell argues that the Northern Territory is what it appears to be; this conjoining legitimates its reality, desire has been displaced.

The lack of reality in the Northern Territory, the gap between appearance and reality, the gap of desire, is a long standing *topos* of the discourse of the Northern Territory. Banjo Paterson uses it in his piece on the Northern Territory published in the *Bulletin* in 1898 (Paterson, 1898). He introduces it in a discussion of the discovery of 'rubies' which turn out to be worthless stones. He goes on to write of the Territory as having:

> leagues and leagues of magnificent country – with no water. Miles and miles of splendidly watered country – where the grass is sour, rank, and

worthless. Mines with rich ore – that it doesn't pay to treat. Quantities of precious stones – that have no value. (Paterson, 1898:365)

Interwoven with the appearance/reality *topos* here are two other *topoi* to which we must return: failure and nature. Paterson constructs his argument in terms of a benign appearance which gives way to a disturbing reality. Nature, as was noted earlier, tends to have negative connotations in Australia's discourse. Here, for Paterson, the fantasy of desire is that nature will be what it appears to be. In Australia's discourse the north is never what it appears to be. Donovan in *At the Other End of Australia* (1984), a sequel to his *A Land Full of Possibilities* (1981), writes that, 'The major theme running through this account is the constant gulf between "perception" and "reality"' (Donovan, 1984:xiv). Donovan, here, is troping the *topos* of deceptive appearance and constructing a thematic, empirical history of the Northern Territory as the difference between appearance, troped in humanist terms as perception, and reality. Paterson's fantasy of the Northern Territory is a primary producer's paradise – magnificent country, plenty of water, mines with rich ore. The Northern Territory is the site of desire, in this image the primary producer's desire. At the limit of Australia's discourse the repressed, the unreal, meets the real. Donaldson tropes this structure into an empirical history.

The gap between appearance and reality in the Northern Territory articulates itself through the *topos* of failure. Indeed so naturalized is the *topos* of failure that, when the Northern Territory is given any history of its own at all, this is the form it takes. The *topos* of failure pervades Paterson's article on the Northern Territory. For example, he writes that 'There's a curse on all NT undertakings' (Paterson, 1898:364). He then lists the failures of pastoralism, sugar plantation, and quinine growing. The Northern Territory is both the site of failure and has a history constituted of failure. The short-lived nature of a number of early white colonizations of the north Australian coast is constructed in histories such as that of Shaw as a succession of failures. Shaw writes, 'Up to 1850 various attempts had been made to establish trading posts in the north: Melville Island, Raffles Bay and Port Essington alike had been abandoned' (Shaw, 1972:169). Such a perception of the early history of the Northern Territory provides the basis for the deployment of a history which moves oppositionally to the dominant Australian historical discourse of progress/expansion/development.[3] These failures (and others such as the 'failure' of the overland telegraph to help populate the north) may be understood as failures to realize the north, hiatuses which forestall progress. Historical writing about the Northern Territory also emphasizes the cyclone of 1897, sometimes the cyclone of 1937, the bombing by the Japanese during 1942, and the cyclone of 1974. Both during the Second World War and after 1974's Cyclone Tracy there were major evacuations of people from Darwin. These events have tended to be constructed as ends to progress, rather than, for example, as periods of consolidation before further expansion. They are constructed as events which both lose the continuity necessary for progress and signal once again the failure of Northern Territory development. A good example of such a history is the popularly oriented *Northern Territory* by Ronald Rose (1966). (In the history section it has a series of running titles one part of which reads 'Pioneer Missionaries; Problems of Development; The Railway That Never Was; Worst Cyclone; Valiant Defeat; The Commonwealth Takes Control': 32–7.)

Darwin's various evacuations (after the first Japanese bombing, and Cyclone Tracy) bear a particular rhetoric – indeed the evacuations themselves were at least partly the product of rhetorical constructions. Such evacuations emphasize the Northern Territory in its position as an outpost, a frontier. The evacuations were to the south, back to a reality which claims itself as civilization. Both the cyclones and the bombing are constructed by way of two major *topoi* of Northern Territory discourse. The cyclones are a part of Nature in its most alien, negative form as The Tropics and the bombing comes from the Other outside of Australia, 'Asia'. Both these historical 'facts', the cyclone and the bombing, are used to reassert the difference of the Northern Territory from the rest of 'Australia'. It is 'forgotten' that cyclones often cross the north Queensland Pacific coast and that Broome, among other places, was also bombed by the Japanese. The construction of hiatuses in Northern Territory history is aided by the view of cyclones as unique events. Both the cyclones and the bombing enter 'Australia' from the north, from beyond the place constituted as the frontier. As a consequence the north is signalled as weak, its reality in question.

The two major cyclones in Darwin's history (major in terms of material destruction caused), and the number of minor ones, are not constructed as a part of a weather pattern which provides continuity but rather are perceived as unique events which occur at irregular intervals. They, like the bombings, are constructed as elements of an invasive Other. An illustration of this can be found in the linkage of Cyclone Tracy with the bombing of Darwin and 'Asia' through the comparison of the devastation caused by Tracy with that caused by the atomic bomb on Hiroshima. This comparison, which has become quite a common one in Northern Territory discourse, can be found in Alan Stretton's autobiography where he writes: '[Group Captain Hitchens] gave me his impression of the damage to the city and the full impact and scope of the catastrophe became frighteningly clear – he said that he had seen Hiroshima soon after the atomic attack and Darwin looked very much the same' (Stretton, 1978: 254–5). In this way cyclones are rhetorically constructed as alien, threatening events coming from outside the limits of Australia, outside Australia's discourse.

With the Northern Territory constructed as a frontier, evacuation becomes a reasonable response to invasion in an area of weakness, of weak reality. Thus, for example, Keneally in his discussion of the first Japanese bombing of Darwin, in his popular delineation of the Northern Territory called *Outback*, gives us this narrative:

There was immediate panic among the forces that had not been directly engaged in dealing with the Japanese and among the civilian population.

People swept out of town on the road to Adelaide River. An Australian airforce officer noticed a Chinaman on a bicycle-driven ice-cream cart. "Where are you going?" he asked the Chinaman. "Melbourne", the Chinaman told him genially. In fact one Australian airforce serviceman did flee as far as that, a distance of 4,000 kilometres. (Keneally, 1983:72)

The frontier, the limit of discourse, the site of repression, is a dangerous place.

Panic is a term applied both to the 1942 evacuation and to the 1974 evacuation. Keneally describes the effect of Cyclone Tracy in the same terms: 'People who lived on the Stuart Highway running south of Darwin showed astounding open-handedness to the panic-stricken refugees' (Keneally, 1983:76). Such rhetoric, which reinforces the preoccupation with evacuation, can be compared with Stretton's comment that, in organizing the airborne evacuation, he found himself one day with 8,000 aircraft seats and only 700 people wanting to leave. As a consequence Stretton ended up offering return tickets to those who wanted a 'holiday' in the south of the country! (Stretton, 1978:270). The rhetoric of panic and evacuation sits well with the image of a frontier, a limen where order is always near to the edge of disorder, understood as loss of law, loss of integration, loss of personal and social control. This is a discursive image of disorder which can be located historically at least as far back as Hobbes' work. Keneally, with his novelist's sense of a story which will resonate, tells us of the fleeing Chinaman, an 'Asian' who is an 'Australian' fleeing 'Asia'. The 'ludicrousness' of the man's attempt to travel 4,000 kilometres in a pedal cart signals, for Australians, the geographical, and of course mythic, distance back to the 'real' Australia of Melbourne. The lack of a railway means that the Stuart Highway provides the link with the real Australia. In Australia's discourse while railways connect, roads emphasize distance. Besides, in Keneally's story, the Chinaman would first have to go to Adelaide – that is where the Stuart Highway goes. However, as we have seen, Adelaide is not as 'real' as Melbourne. The Stuart Highway, then, also signals the separation. Sydney and Melbourne are so far away.[4]

Darwin, then, is constructed as an insecure outpost as opposed to a real city. Real cities have permanence, fixity. They also have permanent, stable populations. The physical destruction and the evacuations signal Darwin's transience as a city. The attempts, after both major evacuations, to (re)construct the material city Darwin by way of a single unified plan demonstrate another southern attempt to realize the north through an assertion of permanence. In this case though a totally planned physical city would itself be an expression of integration. The reference for such a city in Australia is Canberra, an artificial pre-planned city built as the site for the Federal Parliament of Australia. Canberra is the material expression of the integration of Australian society. Keneally, again, recognizes the preoccupation with the permanence of Darwin. He calls Darwin 'the un-lasting city' (Keneally, 1983: title of ch. 5) and ends his chapter on Darwin by writing, 'But for a city that would prefer to be thought of as permanent, a six-year cycle of threat is perhaps too regular'. (The threat referred to here is the average length of time between cyclones.)[5]

There is, in addition, another form of transience attributed to Darwin. This is a transience of population. The rhetoric of Darwin is not only of a city which is transient but of a population which is also. Keneally brings both forms of transience together when he writes that:

> Whatever its name [Palmerston or Darwin] Darwin has always had a transient air. Despite its large hotels and regional patriotism of its Australian/English/Greek/Chinese/Timorese/Lebanese/Vietnamese/Yugoslav/Italian residents, it has always looked, and still looks, like a temporary cantonment for exiles. (Keneally, 1983 : 67)

Darwin's population mix is implicitly compared with that of the real Australian cities the populations of which are still dominated by people of British and Irish extraction. The *topos* of the importance of the population is located in claims of a high migrant population from outside Australia as well as a large number of short-term residents – some for only as long as the Dry – from elsewhere in Australia. One consequence of this is that the overall size of Darwin's population also tends to be much more volatile than that of a real city. In this context the evacuations of Darwin can be understood as extreme examples of the city's construction as having a high level of transience which, again, signals the difference of Darwin from the 'real' cities of Sydney and Melbourne and produces an interesting relation to the Territory's Aboriginal population. In the March 1987 edition of *Land Rights News* there was an article entitled 'Would the real nomads please stand up?' which, by emphasizing the transient nature of much of the white Northern Territory population, was able to describe the effect on the country as a 'high tech slash and burn economy' (*Land Rights News*, 1987:15). The argument is that the Northern Territory Aboriginal population may well be transient, nomadic, but it is pretty much so only within the Northern Territory. By contrast the non-Aboriginal population tends to come and go from places all over Australia. In this way the dominant Australian discourse of a fixed population and continuous land use as a legitimation for occupation of the continent is subverted by white, colonial transience in the Northern Territory.

Keneally's book self-consciously sets out to construct the Northern Territory as different. In his foreword to the book Keneally writes of the 'astounding country' and of the men and women who live their 'extraordinary lives' there (Keneally, 1983:8) Keneally constructs his book on the unreality of the Northern Territory. He calls it *Outback*, the term used to designate land away from the urban civilization of the real, coastal cities. For Keneally the outback includes Darwin. In the Northern Territory the outback includes not only the inland but the coast and the city which is not a real city. Northern Territory car licence plates themselves carry the phrase 'N.T. – Outback Australia'.

In 1915 Elsie Masson published her account of life in the Northern

Territory. It was entitled *An Untamed Territory: The Northern Territory of Australia* (1915). Masson describes the reaction of a woman's friends when they discover that she is going to the Northern Territory:

'Surely you are not going to take the children to that awful hole?' most of her women friends exclaim, with a look which expresses plainly what a heartless mother they think her. Then follows a description of her future home as a burning land, full of fevers and insect pests, where food is bad and health lost after a few years' stay. Darwin itself is represented as a shadeless sun-blistered township, baking all day on a bare rock. (Masson, 1915:26)

Masson then goes on to describe how, subsequently, another woman will tell her that Darwin 'is a Paradise'. Here we can see again the appearance/reality confusion. Darwin and the Northern Territory are constructed at the limit of discourse as either 'an awful hole', Hell we might say, or Paradise. In Masson the two dominant *topoi* for this construction are nature and climate, *topoi* which are interrelated and find their fullest interrelation in the term 'the tropics'.

As the south of Australia became more colonized, more realized, the fantasies about the environment were increasingly confined to the north and were reinforced by the *topos* of 'the tropics'. Paterson, writing for a Sydney/Melbourne audience in the *Bulletin*, begins his piece:

Far in the north of Australia lies a little-known land, a vast half-finished sort of region, wherein Nature has been apparently practising how to make better places. (Paterson, 1898:363)

The land is little known, and little realized in terms of empirical assumptions about knowledge, therefore it can be the site of unreality and so it is. The Northern Territory, in this description, is claimed as not fully realized, it is only half-finished by Nature. Masson reworks the *topos* by claiming the Territory as 'untamed'. The Australian environment has long been experienced as alien and uncomforting. White sums up Dampier's description of the Australian environment by writing:

On each occasion his descriptions of the land, its flora, fauna and inhabitants, were more detailed but just as unfavourable as those of the Dutch. Like them he was full of complaints. The land was barren and fly-pestered; the water was brackish if any could be found; the trees were stunted and bore no fruit; and the animals that might provide food were not plentiful. (White, 1981:2)

From Dampier on, the relation of whites to nature in Australia has been constructed as antagonism, war. Often nature is constructed rhetorically as a wild animal. This metaphor of the Northern Territory as a wild animal runs through Masson's short history of the Northern Territory in her Introduction. The effect of the building of the Overland Telegraph, of the increase in communication, leaves the Territory emerging from the 'battle' of its building badly wounded (Masson, 1915:23). A little further on

DARWIN, TOP OF AUSTRALIA,
The Playground at the End of the Rainbow

Darwin as 'hell' is transformed in touristic discourse as 'paradise'. (By kind permission of N.T. Souvenirs, Pty Ltd.)

Masson suggests that the Northern Territory will 'fight hard, and some prophesy that it will triumph again; but for the most part those who watch the struggle feel that the old warrior has met its match' (Masson, 1915:24). The 'death' of the Northern Territory as an animal will be the birth of the Territory as a real, integrated part of Australia. Masson's description of the Northern Territory as a wild animal is analogous to another Paterson article describing buffalo shooting in the Territory (Paterson, 1899).

Paterson, writing from within the Australian pioneer myth, celebrates what he views as the lack of civilization of the Territory. This lack, which positions the Territory on the frontier, the limit of Australia's discourse, allows it to be a land of fantasy. Paterson writes that, 'some say [the Territory] will be civilised and spoilt; but up to the present it has triumphantly overthrown all who have attempted to improve it' (Paterson, 1898:395). In his buffalo-hunting piece, the animal itself takes on this quality of the Northern Territory:

> It was found that the strength of the buffaloes was so great and their vitality so wonderful that half a dozen bullets would not stop them, but at last the shooters discovered that a bullet fired into the loins from above would paralyse their hindquarters and cause the animal to drop in its tracks. (Paterson, 1899:310)

Here the animal is like the Territory as, in Masson's book, the Territory is like a wild animal. The metonymic quality of Paterson's complex construction of buffalo and Northern Territory 'nature' runs through Northern Territory discourse.

As noted earlier, tourism marks an important moment in the making safe, the realization, of the frontier. In recent tourist literature the wild, antagonistic construction of the Territory's nature, a construction which parallels its formulation as untamed, and therefore as unreal, has been sanitized and reconstructed in traditional Romantic terms. Thus:

> To the east and south of Darwin, scenic features abound. The beautiful Kakadu National Park with its Arnhem Land escarpment, waterfalls, cave paintings and wildlife is a viewing must. (*Outback Australia*, n/d)

In this reconstruction the untamed nature has been tamed. It is now 'scenic' and 'beautiful'. Some of it, made safe within discourse by being made real, is literally patrolled because it has been made a National Park. Perhaps the most well-known example of the reconstruction of Territory nature is to be found in the film *Crocodile Dundee*. The tourist brochure goes on, 'Once an isolated Australian frontier, Darwin and the Top End today provide a vital link in the future of all Australia.' (*Outback Australia*, n/d). In this sentence we find the Territory made safe by being no longer the frontier – even if the brochure is entitled *Outback Australia*. In addition, the integration and realization of the Territory is emphasized in a slippage into the rhetoric of progressive history in which Darwin and the Top End are not only linked to the rest of Australia but to the future of 'all' Australia.

As a part of the deployment of touristic rhetoric the fauna also are made safe. Buffalo and crocodiles are beginning to be farmed. Crocodiles, which have signified the threat of Northern Territory's nature by means of stories of people being taken and eaten, are now visitable by tourists at a farm 40 kilometres out of Darwin and are to be found 'smiling' in welcome in cartoon form on postcards. One radio advertisement for the Crocodile Farm invites people to pop down and visit the crocodiles and 'keep the snappy chappies happy!' Perhaps the final signifier of the domestication of the buffalo and crocodile can be found in the fact that they are both now being popularized as foods. Tourism operates as a mode of integration. It provides the opportunity, the space, for the realization of desire. It is a manifestation of the making safe of desire. In the general realization of Australia the site of such a making safe of desire, of a movement from *jouissance* to *plaisir*, is moving north, from Queensland to the Northern Territory.

The difference of the Top End, specifically, is most clearly signalled in the rhetoric of the tropics. The definition of the tropics as a physical area is very longstanding. It is a definition based on astronomical observations of the apparent movement of the sun, not on climate at all. This is not the place to discuss the transposition of an astronomical definition into a climatic one, but it is important to note some of the dominant connotations which the tropics have acquired in the process: heat, luxuriant growth, sensuality, and a general construction of being different, Other, a place which threatens civilization by promoting lassitude over work, and a general degeneration in social etiquette. One aspect of the rhetoric of the tropics as Other has already

This motel, which is three-quarters built, is in the shape of a crocodile. It is situated in Jabiru in the Kakadu National Park. (Photo by Barry Ledwidge)

been discussed, the cyclones which since at least post-seventeenth-century British discourse – that is since the British intervention in the Carribbean – have been one signal of the difference of the tropics.[6] The cyclones in Australia's north come down with the monsoon, out of the Other, from beyond the limit of discourse. The cyclones signal another (of many) fractures in the attempt to claim Australia's climate as in any way the climate of Britain. A further constituent of the difference of the tropics is heat. In spite of the fact that Darwin's average daytime temperature for both the Wet and the Dry (a white construction of the climate) does not exceed 35°C the tropics are constructed as very hot. When Darwin's humidity rises, increasing people's propensity to sweat, it is constructed in terms of an increase in heat. What we have here is, no doubt, a rhetorical echo of the western geographical notion of a torrid zone around the equator, a notion stretching back to before Pliny.

In Australia's discourse the tropics are most easily discussed in the context of population and acclimatization.[7] For example Taylor, in an article entitled, 'Geographical factors controlling the settlement of tropical Australia', published in 1918, wrote that:

In my own experience, I have passed through the stage necessary to accustom an Englishman from Sheffield (which has an annual temperature of 48°F) to the climate of Sydney (with an annual temperature of 63°F). This is merely a matter of a few years – though longer for middle-aged folk. A lesser period is necessary for the Englishman in Melbourne – none at all in Hobart. But when the uniformly hot climate of the tropics is entered, a very different period of acclimatisation is needed. (Taylor, 1918 : 57)

Taylor argues that no settlers have yet become acclimatized to the North Queensland coast. The period of time he seems to envisage for acclimatization would seem to be generations. At this point we can see how the rhetoric of a white Australia populated from Britain is complicated by the image of part of Australia's climate as different. As a consequence, as late as 1963 Bolton begins his book on North Queensland with the sentence: 'North Queensland is undoubtedly the most successful example in the British Commonwealth of settlement in the tropics by Europeans' (Bolton, 1970: vii). This statement bears the weight of a century of debate in Australia about the ability of the 'white race' to live in 'the tropics' and the concern with the possible debilitating effects of living there.

The origins of the debate over the effects of the climate can be found in a more general debate about the ability of the British to preserve the quality of their race in the new colony of Australia. This debate, White suggests, can be traced back to the Social Darwinist concerns which flowed from Darwin's *The Origin of Species* published in 1859 (White, 1981 : 68–72). Such general concerns about the possible degeneration of British stock in Australia appear to have been fading by the early years of the twentieth century – fading, that is, in relation to the southern part of Australia.[8] Such a decrease in concern signals a shift in attitude towards the climate which reconstructs it as 'normal', as similar enough to the British climate not to have antipathetic consequences on the migrant population. However, the further north one moved in Australia the further one moved out of such an acceptable climate.

The category of 'the tropics' stands as an extreme environment when compared to temperate climes within this formulation, and the Sydney/ Melbourne axis is included by virtue of claiming it to have a tolerable climate. Consequently, in the 1940s we still encounter the proposition that whites cannot colonize 'the tropics'. Elkin, Professor of Anthropology at Sydney University, for example, argued, in a paper entitled 'Is white Australia doomed?' which was part of a symposium on white Australia held in January 1946 and published in 1947, that:

[Recent research] shows that there are parts of Queensland quite suitable for Caucasians, for example, north to Rockhampton. Some other parts, such as Mackay and Townsville are suitable provided the necessary adaption is made in summer. Other parts again, like Cardwell, Cairns and Cloncurry are only suitable for specially selected persons, who, in addition must make marked adaptions in their way of life, housing and clothing; and fourthly, regions like Burketown and Cape York are not suitable for continuous habitation by Caucasians. (Elkin, 1947 : 195–6)

The recent research referred to by Elkin was a paper published by Professor

D. H. K. Lee in 1940 through the Department of Physiology, University of Queensland. Elkin presents a geographical spread of an increasingly alien climate along a north/south gradation ignoring, with the exception of Cloncurry and possibly of Burketown, the inland climates of Australia. The result is that we are presented with a series of graduated steps north towards 'the tropics' where Elkin refers to Lee as doubting whether a Caucasian 'population can maintain physical and mental activity and efficiency quite on a par with sub-tropical or temperate climes' (Elkin, 1947 : 196). This kind of argument operates discursively to produce Darwin and the Top End as a geographical/discursive space which, in population and the life of that population, must be fundamentally different to the rest of Australia. In fact Elkin does not mention the Top End of the Territory at all. Once more, it, and specifically here its white population, have been repressed in the discourse.

One practical effect of the debate over climate can be found in the tracing of the regulations on which the White Australia policy was founded. These regulations seem always to have been applied later, and more laxly, in the Northern Territory than elsewhere.[9] This is usually accounted for in terms of the need for labour in the Northern Territory to build, for example, the Overland Telegraph and Pine Creek railway. However when we remember how apparently unsuitable 'the tropics' were understood to be for Caucasians another reason becomes possible. Elkin, in fact, suggests the possibility of peopling the north with races more adapted to the climate, (those from southern Europe or the Orient are the terms he uses: Elkin, 1947 : 195–6), a solution inimical to the prevailing assimilationist policy of the time.

An alternative possibility was put forward by Taylor in 1918: 'It is the race fusion which has made Latin America possible' (Taylor, 1918 : 55). The possibility of a new mixed race was proposed again by Mr Justice E. A. Douglas in the discussion of Elkin's paper:

> There is a good deal to be said against the white population having to live in such surroundings [Torres Straits and Suez], but I cannot see that we can populate the far north unless we have some other mixture with the Anglo-Saxon race. We cannot resist the introduction of other races into tropical Australia – and tropical Australia is about half of Australia.' (Borrie, 1947 : 203)

'The tropics', then, is not only different from the rest of Australia, it marks a necessary opening in the discourse of white Australia. 'The tropics' signals the limit, geographical and ideological, of white racism. In Taylor's and Douglas' remarks the miscegenetic solution is articulated in the context of assimilation. The rhetoric, which we have already noted, of Darwin's racially plural population, sits equally well, if not better, with the more recent concern of multiculturalism. In this context Darwin's claim to a heterogeneous cosmopolitan population places it once more on the limits of discourse, as being what Sydney/Melbourne would like to be. In some recent tourist literature for Fannie Bay Gaol Museum we are told that: 'The history of Fannie Bay Gaol is however, in part, the history of a small, remote European administration trying to impose its own judicial code on a cosmopolitan population' (*Fannie Bay Gaol Museum*, n/d). Such a history signals the difference of the Northern Territory from the rest of Australia and identifies that difference in a cosmopolitanism made acceptable through the rhetoric of multiculturalism. Darwin, then, and the Northern Territory, retain their position on the limit of Australia's discourse both as different and as the site of desire. Once again, however the difference is made safe.

The Northern Territory figures the limits of an Australian discursive system. The Northern Territory, the least real part of the discourse of Australia, has historically provided the site for the repressed Other of the real Australia. In this sense the Territory has been constituted binarily in relation to the rest of Australia. It is constructed as isolated compared to the rest of Australia which is viewed as internally cohesive. It is a place of failure to set against the success of the rest of Australia. It is a place that lacks population and economic development to set against the populated, developed rest of Australia. It is climatically alien as against the acceptable southern climate, and it is the frontier, the limit of civilisation to set against the civilized south of the country. Underpinning all these the Northern Territory is the site of appearance, the place of the unreal against which the rest of Australia can measure its reality. We need to note how, for over a hundred years, the production of the Northern Territory by the rest of Australia has remained remarkably static.[10] We need to note also how, as the Territory now produces itself as a tourist site, it reworks the traditional imagery into 'safer', more real terms. Thus, for example, the claimed mental degeneration and lassitude which was considered to be an effect of tropical living is reworked into the idea of the Top End as having a relaxing atmosphere. Historically the Territory has been the manifestation of the repressed for the real 'Australia'. It has been the weakest moment in the discourse. It has also been the moment when the Other of 'Australia' meets the Other against which 'Australia' defines itself, 'Asia', embodied in the 'Asian threat'. Beyond the Other of repression is another Other outside of the discourse, outside of repression which can amalgamate with, and is given form by, the Others of repression which construct Australia's discourse. The patrolling, the safety claimed by the patrolling, inherent in tourism is a beginning of the consolidation of Australia's discourse and the realization of the Northern Territory.

Notes

I should like to thank the staff of the Special Collections section of Darwin Institute of Technology for their help in facilitating the gathering of material for this article. I should also like to thank Kris Bradley for all her work word-processing this article through its many stages whilst being extremely busy with other tasks.

1 An earlier example of the rhetorical construction of the Northern Territory in the terms I am about to discuss here can be found in Fraser, (1910).

2 Powell notes this also: (1982 : 241).

3 Abbott, (1954 : 7), argues for the importance of development in the Northern Territory. Abbott was once Administrator of the Territory.

4 The other major link with the south of Australia is constructed similarly. This is the Overland Telegraph which connected Darwin with Java and Port Augusta in 1872. Shaw describes the event like this: 'In 1872 [South Australia] built a telegraph to Darwin at a cost of £400,000, arguing that this would "promote the occupation of large tracts in the interior". But not even the ability to send messages at a shilling a word brought settlers' (Shaw, 1972 : 169). Once again we find here the rhetoric of failure. This time it is linked to communication. The telegraph, it is implied, was simply not enough communication to realize the Northern Territory, to bring it within Australia's discourse as a manifest entity. This trope is transposed in terms of the failure to populate. In Australia's colonial inflection to its discourse peopling by whites is a mode of realization. It is interesting how well, in white Australian discourse, the idea that whites ended the Aboriginal dreamtime fits with this formulation.

5 There is here the implicit possibility of normalizing cyclones in Northern Territory discourse by accepting their regularity.

6 One source for this history is Hulme, (1981).

7 There is a long history of literature on this topic. In addition to what I quote from here there is, for example, a lengthy article by Breinl & Young, (1920). See also Barrett, (1925). Cilento (1925) contributes to the debate by arguing that climate as such plays no part in the ability of white people to live in the tropics. He writes that: 'For a considerable time it has been more and more apparent that the question of the possibility of establishing the white man in tropical countries, possessing no large resident native population, is infinitely more largely a question of preventive medicine than a question of climate' (Introduction, p. 5). One of Cilento's main opponents was the American, Ellsworth Huntington, who argued a climatic determinist position in such works as (1925) and (1929).

8 There is a parallel to be drawn between the loss of fear of the degeneration of the white race in the south of the country and the gradual imposition of the White Australia Policy.

9 This can be traced in Willard (1967). See for example pp. 65–6, 71–4, 104–5. The positive attitude towards Chinese within the Territory is typified by Searcy (1909), ch. 22. Searcy was sub-collector of customs at Port Darwin for fourteen years.

10 The discourses of other 'new' countries such as America – with California as its frontier – operate similarly. The frontier marks the site of repression, the limit of presence. However the frontier is inflected differently in different national discourses. In America, for example, the frontier, a myth which has been explored for a long time, has been constituted in relation to a nature that has positive connotations. From within this context the frontier is formulated as the site of challenge. In Australia, on the other hand, where nature has negative connotations, much effort is spent consolidating the frontier. A general introduction to empirical debates about the frontier can be found in Lipset (1968).

Bibliography

Abbott, Charles (1950), *Australia's Frontier Province*, Sydney: Angus & Robertson.
Barrett, James (1925), 'Tropical Australia', *United Empire*, 16, pp. 37–43.

Bolton, Geoffrey (1970), *A Thousand Miles Away*, Canberra: Australian University Press (originally published 1963).

Breinl, A. and Young, W. J. (1920), 'Tropical Australia and its settlement', *Annals of Tropical Medicine and Parasitology*, 13 (1920), pp. 351–412.

Cilento, Raphael (1925), *The White Man in the Tropics*, Melbourne.

Clark, Manning (1962–3), *A History of Australia*, Carlton Vic: Melbourne University Press.

Clark, Manning (1964), *A Short History of Australia*, London: Heinemann.

Donovan, Peter (1981), *A Land Full of Possibilities*, Brisbane: University of Queensland Press.

Donovan, Peter (1984), *At the Other End of Australia*, Brisbane: University of Queensland Press.

Elkin, Adolphus (1947), 'Is Australia doomed?', in Wilfred Borrie et. al.

Elkin, Adolphus (ed.) (1947), *A White Australia*, Sydney: Australasian Publishing.

Fannie Bay Gaol Museum (n.d. c. 1988), Northern Territory Museum and Art Galleries Board.

Fitzgerald, Ross (1982), *A History of Queensland: From the Dreaming to 1915*, St Lucia: Queensland University Press.

Fitzgerald, Ross, (1984), *A History of Queensland: From 1915 to the Early 1980s*, St Lucia: Queensland University Press.

Fraser, John Foster (1910), *Australia: the Making of a Nation*, London: Cassell.

Hancock, William (Keith) (1966), *Australia*, Brisbane: Jacaranda (originally published 1930).

Hill, Ernestine (1951), *The Territory*, Sydney: Angus & Robertson.

Holmes, Macdonald (1963), *Australia's Open North*, Sydney: Angus & Robertson.

Hulme, Peter (1981), 'Hurricanes in the Caribbees: the constitution of the discourse of English colonialism', in Francis Barker *et al.* (eds), *1642: Literature and Power in the Seventeenth Century*, Colchester: University of Essex.

Huntington, Ellsworth (1925), *West of the Pacific*, New York.

Huntington, Ellsworth (1929), 'Natural selection and climate in Northern Australia', *Economic Record*, November, pp. 185–201.

Keneally, Thomas (1983), *Outback*, Sydney: Hodder & Stoughton.

Land Rights News (1987), 'Would the real nomads stand up?' 2, 2 (March).

Lipset, Seymour (1968), 'The Turner thesis in comparative perspective. An introduction', in Richard Hofstader and Seymour Lipset (eds), *Turner and the Sociology of the Frontier*, New York: Basic Books.

Masson, Elsie (1915), *An Untamed Territory: The Northern Territory of Australia*, London: Macmillan.

Outback Australia n/d c. 1988 The Northern Territory.

Pascoe, Rob (1979), *The Manufacture of Australian History*, Melbourne: Oxford University Press.

Paterson, Andrew Barton ('Banjo') (1898), 'The Cycloon, Paddy Cahill and the G. R.', *Bulletin*, 31 December.

Paterson, Andrew Barton ('Banjo') (1899), 'Buffalo shooting in Australia', *Sydney Mail*, 7 January.

Powell, Alan (1982), *Far Country*, Melbourne: Melbourne University Press.

Rose, Ronald (1966), *Northern Territory*, Sydney: Nelson Doubleday.

Searcy, Alfred (1909), *In Australian Tropics*, Melbourne: Angus & Robertson.

Shaw, Alan (1972), *The Story of Australia*, London: Faber (originally published 1954).

Stretton, Alan (1978), *Soldier in a Storm*, Sydney: Collins.

Taylor, Griffith (1918), 'Geographical factors controlling the settlement of tropical Australia', *Queensland Geographical Journal*, XXXII–XXXIII, 18–19.

Ward, Russel (1958), *The Australian Legend*, Melbourne: Oxford University Press.

White, Richard (1981), *Inventing Australia*, Sydney: Allen & Unwin.

Willard, Myra (1967), *History of the White Australia Policy to 1920*, Melbourne: Melbourne University Press.

DAVID LEE

DISCOURSE: DOES IT HANG TOGETHER?

T he concept of 'discourse' has been used in a variety of ways in current work on linguistic processes operating above the level of the sentence.[1] In this paper I wish to examine one particular use of the term associated most closely with the work of a number of scholars who are concerned with the relationship between linguistic processes and 'ideology' (Fowler *et al.*, 1979, Kress and Hodge, 1979), especially with the way in which the concept has been used by Gunther Kress (Kress 1985a, 1985b, 1985c).

In 'Ideological structures in discourse' Kress defines his position by drawing a sharp distinction between 'discourse' and 'text' in the following terms:

> Discourse is a category that belongs to and derives from the social domain and text is a category that belongs to and derives from the linguistic domain. The relationship between the two is one of realization. Discourse finds its expression in text. However, this is never a straightforward relation; any one text may be the expression of a number of sometimes competing and contradictory discourses.
>
> The notion of a discourse advanced here is that of 'mode of talking', a notion that attempts to capture the quite commonplace insight that is pointed to in expressions such as 'legal discourse', 'racist discourse', 'medical discourse'. (p. 27)

Kress's view that discourse 'belongs to and derives from the social domain' raises questions concerning the relationship between discourse and genre. Kress argues here and elsewhere (1985c : 81–2) that not only do various discourses interact with each other in the production of a text but that genre is also an identifiable component in this process. The difference between the two concepts appears in part to have to do with differences of level. Discourses derive from large-scale social institutions, such as medicine; genre derives from the specific social occasions associated with such institutions. The difference in level is highlighted by the claim that discourse (unlike genre) is directly related to ideology in the sense that 'social institutions produce specific ways of talking about certain areas of social life, which are related to the place and nature of that institution' (p. 28). In this way certain boundaries are imposed with respect to what may and what may not be said in that area of social life, constraints which can be described as ideological.

For the linguist the interesting claim here is that these principles of organization are said to have consequences for linguistic structure:

> Certain syntactic forms will necessarily correlate with certain discourses. . . . For instance, in discourses of power and authority, social agency will be assigned in particular ways and this will be expressed through particular transitivity forms; or specific modal forms will systematically express relations of power. (p. 28)

There is of course a longstanding debate in linguistics over the nature of the relationship between ideology and language. Much of this debate has focused on a question that will not be taken up here – the question of whether language is a determinant of ideology (the best-known proponents of this view being Whorf and Sapir) or whether the reverse relationship holds. In general Kress appears to espouse the latter view: 'The defined and delimited set of statements that constitute a discourse are . . . expressive of and organized by a specific ideology' (p. 30); although at other points a rather different (but not a Whorfian) view appears: 'ideology and discourse are aspects of the same phenomenon, regarded from two different standpoints' (p. 30).

For my purposes here the important questions have to do with the concept of correlation. On the one hand there is clearly an idea in the work of all of those who have explored the relationship between ideology and language that there is what can be characterized as a 'vertical' correlation between the principles according to which knowledge is organized and the forms of language which shape or reflect those principles. On the other hand a different kind of correlation is implied both by the concept ideology and by the concept discourse, a correlation which can be seen as operating in the horizontal plane between different components of the ideology or discourse rather than in the vertical plane that relates cognition to language. That is, the concept ideology postulates a correlation between the various components which constitute a particular ideology. Similarly, the concept of discourse is based on the proposition that there are correlations between linguistic processes, such that the operation of one process in a given discourse will tend to be associated with the operation of other specifiable processes. These horizontal correlations between linguistic features follow from the vertical relationship between discourse and ideology, since the processes that constitute a given discourse, although they may appear to be somewhat disparate in narrowly linguistic terms, operating in all components (semantic, syntactic, phonological) of the linguistic system, are nevertheless functionally related. The factor that binds them together is precisely their role as the mediator of the associated ideology. Within this framework, the central issue is whether the kind of horizontal correlations between linguistic processes postulated by the discourse model do in fact characterize textual structure and if so at what level of analysis. This question is inextricably bound up with that concerning the vertical relationship between ideology and language. That is, the issue is whether the textual exponents of a given discourse do in fact possess the kind of functional homogeneity which the discourse model attributes to them.

The kind of questions raised here clearly cannot be discussed in the abstract – they can only be explored in the context of an analysis of particular texts. The first text I will use is also used by Kress (1985b) to illustrate the concept of discourse. My argument is that the correlative structures he postulates in this case do not in fact hold, or at least that the structures in question are much looser than he suggests. This proposition is based on the view that the linguistic processes in question are functionally more heterogeneous than has been claimed. At one level this can be interpreted as a relatively minor disagreement over exemplification. My second text, for a number of reasons concerning the nature of the social context in which the text is embedded, and the nature of the ideology from which it derives, seems to constitute a much clearer exemplar. However, in this case too, I will argue that the discourse model has only a limited applicability; that a fine-grained analysis again leads to a much more complex picture of the factors underlying textual structure than the model suggests. This disagreement over the relative usefulness of the concept of discourse and the related concept of ideology should not be allowed to obscure the fact that my argument accepts and is based on the idea pioneered by Kress and his associates concerning the importance of functional processes in the analysis of texts.

To illustrate the correlative structures that are said to constitute a particular discourse, Kress (1985b) cites the following text, a television news item broadcast by an Adelaide commercial station during the 1981 tour of New Zealand by the South African Rugby Union team, the Springboks.

Verbal text	*Visual text*
Newsreader: The first match of the highly controversial Springbok tour of NZ produced two victors today: the South Africans and the police.	Head of newsreader
The Springboks had the easier of the clashes annihilating a Poverty Bay rugby side 24 to 6. But the NZ police forces guarding the ground at Gisbourne had to cope with dozens of angry protesters who chanted anti-apartheid slogans, blew whistles to disrupt the match, and made two attempts to invade the pitch. Here's today's special satellite report:	Slow motion background picture of punch

Reporter 1: Things began peacefully enough with a march through the town. But the calm wasn't to last for long. Squads of police hurried to the vulnerable back fence but reinforcements weren't there quickly enough. The demonstrators stormed the fence, with only a handful of police trying to hold them back. Many managed to get up a slippery bank and began tearing the fence down. Violent clashes followed. More clashes, this time more bitter, erupted. The confrontation was to last several hours. Several people claimed to have been injured in the brawls. As some lay on the ground, emotion subsided. The demonstration ended late this afternoon after 13 had been arrested.	March head-on; close up of Maori face, shot from behind police lines Back fence
	Close up of fights; Focus on punch being thrown
	Injured person Arrest
	Arrest
Reporter 2: Elsewhere around the country many other people were arrested. Demonstrations such as this one in Auckland this evening spanned the length and breadth of the nation today as the anti-tour groups branded today NZ's day of shame. JW reporting from NZ for Eyewitness News.	Head of Reporter 2 in front of demonstration

Kress's discussion focuses on three major properties of the text, including both the verbal and visual codes. The first property has to do with transactivity patterns. A transactive is defined as an event or action which is 'portrayed as arising directly as the result of some agent's action and with a direct effect on a goal' (Kress, 1985b : 34). A non-transactive is an action or event which is 'either a self-caused action or one that happens in some unspecified way'. Examples of transactives cited from the text are *chanted slogans, . . . blew whistles, . . . disrupted the match*; examples of non-transactives are *violent clashes followed, more clashes erupted, the confrontation was to last several hours, emotion subsided*. In an important comment Kress observes:

Clearly the mode in which an action is presented as transactive or non-transactive is not a matter of truth or reality but rather a matter of the way in which that particular action is integrated into the ideological system of the speaker. (p. 34)

Now Kress takes it to be significant that in this text most of the clauses in which an event is presented in the transactive mode have the demonstrators (or some lexical substitute of them) as subjects and agents. Events that are predicated of the demonstrators include . . . *chanted anti-apartheid slogans,* . . . *blew whistles,* . . . *disrupted the match,* . . . *invaded the pitch,* . . . *stormed the fence,* . . *began tearing the fence down,* and so on. By contrast, events in which police are involved are presented either in the non-transactive mode or in a special form of the transactive, the truncated passive, e.g. *13 people had been arrested.* The point here is that the transactive/non-transactive distinction is not a discrete opposition but rather a continuum such that truncated passives, although transactive, are seen as rather low on the scale of transactivity. Another example illustrating this point is *the police had to cope with angry demonstrators.* The presence of the *have to* structure here makes the example much less prototypically transactive than *the police coped with angry demonstrators.*[2] Other non-transactive events in which the police are involved here are . . . *hurried to the back fence, violent clashes followed, more clashes erupted, the confrontation was to last several hours, many other people were arrested.* Kress argues that this distribution of transactives and non-transactives is not accidental. He suggests that the distribution derives from a certain ideological system, presumably one that might be described as an 'anti-demonstrator' or 'anti-protest' ideology, or, at a more general level, a conservative ideology.

This ideology is said to express itself in two other major features of the text. One of these is the pervasive military metaphor with the police *guarding the ground,* the demonstrators *invading the pitch* or *storming the fence* and the two together becoming involved in *violent clashes.* The main function of this metaphor is said to be to enable one of the participants to be cast in the role of friend or defender and the other to be cast in the role of enemy.

The third feature of the text which is said to be a manifestation of the underlying ideology, perhaps its most powerful exponent, is the visual text:

> Camera shots of the demonstrators are taken as head-on, so that they are seen as advances on the police and by implication on the viewer. . . . The visual code operating in the text locates the viewer more precisely and more decisively than the verbal without any need to use overt moralistic, political or ideologically charged labels. (p. 35)

A contrast is drawn with another report on a non-commercial channel, in which camera shots were from side-on to the demonstrators (and in which the verbal text is said to have been characterized by a more equal distribution of transactives and non-transactives across demonstrators and police).

The suggestion that there are correlations between the various textual features identified here is open to question at a number of levels. At the lowest level the question is whether the various manifestations of each category constitute a unitary phenomenon. For example, is there a single explanation for the fact that the various non-transactives in the text all denote processes in which the police are participants? If it turns out to be the case that a variety of unrelated factors are involved here, with some non-transactives attributable to one factor, some to another, then clearly the concept of discourse can be undermined at that level. If, however, we accept that there is a functional unity associated with the various exponents of each category, then the concept of discourse can be challenged at a higher level if it can be shown, for example, that the distribution of transactivity patterns is not in fact determined by the factor that is responsible, say, for the military metaphor. In this example, the concept seems to me to be challengeable at both levels.

Let me begin with the lower-level question of whether the transactivity patterns are functionally unitary. Consider, for example, the relationship between the prototypical non-transactives such as *violent clashes followed* and the less prototypical examples represented by the truncated passives. There are three truncated passives here: *several people claimed to have been injured in the brawls, . . . after 13 had been arrested, elsewhere around the country many other people were arrested.* Kress's point seems to be that the non-specification of an actor in processes such as *injure* and *arrest*, which leads to the selection of a (truncated) passive, mediates an ideology in which the police react to rather than instigate events. However, the factors underlying these structures are surely rather more specific and somewhat more complex than this account suggests. The passive is one of the family of thematic processes in English (Huddleston, 1984 : 437–70) and one important function of the truncated passive is to focus on the process (with non-specification of the actor following from this as a corollary rather than as a motivating factor). That is, these examples can be interpreted as serving to highlight the (results of the) processes of *injure* and *arrest* – an explanation which it is difficult to integrate into the kind of ideology said to be mediated by these structures here. Another factor which clearly facilitates the non-specification of the agent in the case of *arrest* has to do with the pragmatics of the situation – our knowledge of the world imposes very tight restrictions on the range of referents that we normally interpret as agents of this process. In other words, the choice of these truncated passives can be seen to follow from a mix of factors – some of them having to do with thematic processes relating to their position in this particular text ('demonstrators' as theme, 'arrest' and 'injure' as theme), some having to do with pragmatic considerations – rather than from 'ideology' in the sense in which it is used here. This interpretation is in fact more consistent with the way the verbal text interacts with the visual text than the alternative. It would be odd to select structures in the verbal text attempting to undermine the transactive nature of processes in which the police were involved whilst at the same time presenting powerful visual signals expressing a rather different message (policemen fighting with demonstrators, policemen arresting demonstrators and so on).

Let me turn now to the higher-level question of whether the cross-correlation between two of the major discourse components indicated by Kress is in fact defensible. Let us take it that, apart from the truncated passives, the transactivity choices constitute a unitary phenomenon and that the various manifestations of the military metaphor also belong to a single category. The question here, then, is whether these two phenomena derive from a single underlying determinant. Kress suggests that the military metaphor derives from a particular kind of ideology, associated with certain powerful sub-groups within our society. There may, however, be an alternative explanation concerned with very general perceptions of the relationship between the demonstration and the football match. It can be argued that the football match and the demonstration stand in an unmarked/marked opposition, with the football match operating as the unmarked element. The situation can be compared to a proposition such as 'the pen is on the table', where for all kinds of pragmatic reasons we situate the pen (the marked term) with respect to the table (the unmarked term) rather than vice versa (*'The table is under the pen'). Here, quite clearly, it is the demonstration that situates itself with respect to the football match in terms of both the time and place of its occurrence – and indeed its nature (e.g. the whistle-blowing). This factor can be interpreted as the crucial one with respect to the military metaphor – it is this which can be seen to underlie the very general perception, shared by demonstrators and police alike, that it is the football match that is under 'attack'. There may well be other factors operating here too. It seems not irrelevant to note that the football match has an institutional status which is not enjoyed by the demonstration and there are also general perceptions of the police enshrined in such phrases as *the thin blue line* which contribute to the metaphor.[3] It may well be, of course, that these perceptions constitute some kind of ideology in themselves but, if so, it is very different from the one which Kress sees as operating here, since it is not associated with a specific sub-group. It therefore seems to be of doubtful validity to attempt to correlate the military metaphor with other features of the text that are seen as mediating such an ideology.

The idea that there is some general conservative ideology underlying this text is by no means totally implausible and I do not wish to argue against the view that it contributes to certain aspects of textual structure – some aspects of the transactivity choices, for example, and possibly certain characteristics of the visual code. My point is that the correlative patterns which a concept such as discourse presupposes are much weaker than the model suggests. My contention is that, for any text, there will be a vast array of factors engaged in the realizational processes and that only some of these correlate with each other in structures to which concepts such as discourse and genre can plausibly be applied. It may therefore be misleading to argue that texts are the product of the interaction of discourse(s) and genre.

To illustrate this argument further, I turn now to a different text, selected on the basis that it appears to be a particularly difficult one for my position. At first blush this text seems to be a prototypical example of Kress's claim that texts are the product of the interaction of discourse(s) with genre. I will argue, however, that even in this example the elements involved in the realizational processes cannot plausibly be gathered together under these concepts in any fine-grained analysis of textual structure.

The following text was produced within a university context. It is a memorandum sent by the Head of an academic Department to members of his Department.[4]

DEPARTMENT OF . . .

Memorandum to academic staff:

1. STAFF FROM AB/1 TEACHING STAFF WORK LOAD, 19**
   The annual drudgery of setting down a summary of what we do with our time needs to be undertaken again.
   Each staff-member needs to fill in a copy of STAFF FORM AB/1. The purposes of the forms are

   i to enable the Standing Committee to see whether the work-load of the Department is equitably distributed
   ii to enable the Standing Committee to see whether the Department, by comparison with other departments, needs more or fewer staff
   iii to enable the University to indicate to the Universities Commission how it is using its resources. It is the Universities Commission rather than the University that need some of the details requested.

The form is the same as for last year. A few suggestions may, nevertheless, not be unwelcome:

   i read carefully the *notes on the back of the form*
   ii note especially points 9, 10, 25
   iii if you take a class or classes for someone else, please make sure that only one person claims the hour(s)
   iv for second semester, in a subject that contains a lecture programme as well as seminars, the course convener should allocate the 13 (or 26 or . . .) hours of lectures and inform the people involved
   v Do not underestimate, under D, the time needed for University administration including committees. Attendance at Staff meetings probably amounts to 14 hours in the year; attendance at the Board of the Faculty perhaps 6–10 hours; attendance at the Improvements Committee and course sub-committees perhaps 30–40 hours. Consultations with colleagues and students about a current subject should probably appear under B: Associated Work; Other – every subject is likely to require at least 40 hours per semester for this
   vi the total of A+B+C+D should probably fall between 1800 and 2400
   vii please let **** have the completed form by 22 April – earlier if possible.

2. STAFF DUTIES: Second Semester 19**

I had been hoping to defer this schedule until preliminary enrolment figures were available. The need to complete STAFF FORM AB/1 has, however, forced me to allocate staff duties on guess-work enrolments and without the desirable range of consultation. Please let me know of any problems you have with the allocation.

Within the context of the kind of discourse model elaborated by Kress the first and most obvious point about this text is that there appear to be two competing discourses interacting with each other in the genre of 'official memorandum'. These two discourses could be called the discourse of authority (or power) and the discourse of solidarity. Each discourse derives from certain perceptions of aspects of the social structure within which the text is embedded. The discourse of authority derives from the nature of the hierarchical, institutionally-defined relationship between the writer and intended readers of the text, and from the particular function of this text. The discourse of solidarity derives from the writer's perception of a different, egalitarian relationship between himself and his readers which arises from a variety of factors – the similarity of their professional roles as teachers and a certain commonality of interests and duties. (It is perhaps not irrelevant to note that within this institution a Head of Department is in effect elected by colleagues.) The relevant ideology here is one that encompasses these competing perspectives, so that the main problem to be resolved in the construction of the text is that of reconciling the discourse of authority with the discourse of solidarity.

The discourse of authority is characterized here by two major features. The first is the very large number of directive utterances. The second component is the writer's role as purveyor of privileged information, particularly concerning the origin and purpose of the forms. It seems reasonable to surmise that these two components should correlate strongly with each other across many texts, so that the concept 'discourse of authority' might be used to comprise these and related features.

The discourse of solidarity is rather more complex in that it consists of a wide range of semantic and syntactic features, the function of which is to modalize the discourse of authority. This discourse begins strongly with such lexical choices as *drudgery*, the use of the inclusive pronoun forms *we* and *our*, the choice of *need* and the passive *to be undertaken*. *Need* is of some interest here (*the annual drudgery . . . needs to be undertaken again*). The item has a key role in the process of what Fowler *et al.* (1979:38) have called the process of 'mystification' in that it mystifies not only the source of the requirement but also its nature. As far as the source is concerned, the requirement may derive from some source outside the proposition of which it forms a part (in this case 'The University') or from the agent of the associated process (as in the most salient reading of *I need to talk to you*). This latter interpretation is possible even when the agent of the process is not specified, as in the kind of truncated passive which we find here. That is, the interpretation is available that the 'need' to fill in this form is located within the staff member herself/himself. It is, then, the mystification over the source of the requirement together with the associated mystification over its nature (are we dealing with an authority-based imperative or with a personal desire or possibly both?) that serves to mitigate or modalize the expression of directive meaning. The effect of the second sentence in which *need* occurs again, this time as the predicate of *each staff member*, is to make the 'personal source' reading even more easily available and thereby to heighten the mitigatory effect. The item occurs for a third time towards the end of the text (*the need to complete STAFF FORM AB/1 has, however, forced me to allocate* . . .). By this stage the concept, still obscure in terms of its source and nature, has become reified through the grammatical process of nominalization. As a result it can now adopt an agentive role with the writer cast in the role of patient and this serves further to establish an identity between the relationship of writer and that of the addressee to the constructed 'need'.

The mystification over the deontic source associated with *need* is concerned with directionality – does the 'need' impinge on or derive from the individual staff member? A similar mystification over directionality occurs in the clause *a few suggestions may, nevertheless, not be unwelcome*. The characterization of directives as 'suggestions', the use of the modal, and the double negative structure all constitute part of the discourse of solidarity but more interesting are the directionality meanings deriving from *unwelcome*. The function of this item is to assign a certain degree of agentivity to the addressee, so that again the idea of the directionality of the directive *from* the writer *to* the addressee is reversed.

In sum it is arguable that there are a cluster of interrelated features in this text involving semantic operations (e.g. on the directionality of deontic and locutionary processes) and syntactic operations (truncated passives, double negatives, nominalizations and so on). Their interrelatedness stems from the fact that they can be seen to have a unitary function – to modalize the expression of directive meaning. This function derives from the fact that there is an underlying conflict in the social context in which the text is situated between the institutionally-defined hierarchical relationship of writer to addressee(s) and the egalitarian relationship deriving from other aspects of their professional role.

The problem with the discourse model here, however, is that there are other features of the text which are functionally similar to those assigned above to the discourse of solidarity but which derive from factors other than those identified as underlying this discourse. In other words, there are features which appear on one level to constitute part of that discourse, but which at a deeper (or possibly 'finer') level have a much looser correlative tie (if indeed any at all) with those features. This suggests that the danger inherent in the discourse model is that it oversimplifies the nature of the factors determining textual structure. To put it another way, it postulates much tighter correlations between the components governing textual features than those which do in fact exist.

A particular illustration of this point is provided by the use of *please* in directives. Examples are:

- if you take a class or classes for someone else, please make sure that only one person claims the hour(s)
- please let * * * * have the completed form by 22 April
- Please let me know of any problems you have with the allocation.

These directives contrast with such bare imperatives as *read carefully the notes on the back of the form, note especially points 9, 10, 25, do not underestimate under D the time needed for University administration*. It is tempting at first sight to assign the bare imperatives here to the discourse of authority and the *please* imperatives to the discourse of solidarity, given the fact that the function of *please* is clearly to modalize the expression of directive meaning. However, if we look at the contrast between the examples in more detail, we find that a rather different factor from that suggested by the discourse model is at work here. What is striking here is that, although the function of *please* is clearly to mitigate the expression of directive meaning, the effect is not in fact to superimpose solidarity-type meanings on authoritative meanings in the way that other mitigatory elements discussed above operate. If anything, the reverse is the case. The *please* directives are in fact rather more distancing in this case than are the bare imperatives. The important factor involved in the distribution of the two imperative types here seems to have to do with the writer's perception not so much of the relationship between himself and the addressees but of the relationship between the addressees and the specified action. The bare imperative is used when the action is perceived as being in some sense to the benefit of the addressees – where there is a danger, if the action is not performed, of addressees doing themselves less than justice. The *please* directives, on the other hand, tend to be used when the opposite situation applies – when the specified action is of some cost to addressees (e.g. meeting a deadline) or when there is a danger of them gaining some unfair advantage (e.g. claiming to have taught a class which they have not in fact taken). In more general terms the distribution of *please* seems to be connected with the question of 'face' (Goffman, 1967). The bare imperative is used when the specified action is concerned with positive face and the *please* imperative when it is concerned with negative face (Brown and Levinson, 1978 : 66).

It is not at all obvious how this situation can be integrated into the discourse model, especially as the model appears to predict that the distribution of the forms in question should be precisely the opposite of the one observed. The problem is that, since the model derives the various discourses postulated from very general aspects of social structure, it has no way of accounting for the way in which very specific aspects of a particular communicative situation (in this case the relationship of the addressee to a particular action) govern the distribution of linguistic features. There are no doubt many texts in which the distribution of *please* would correlate with features assigned here to the discourse of solidarity – when the question of 'face', for example, was not a central issue in the communicative situation. When it does arise, however, the ties between *please* and the components of the discourse of solidarity are weakened. The point is that we can expect this to apply to those other features assigned to a given discourse. The factors which bear on the selection of a particular linguistic form are various and complex and the factors which cluster together in the production of one text to produce a particular set of linguistic choices will not necessarily cluster together in another in the way that the model suggests.

Another illustration of this point is provided by the distribution of the words *perhaps*, *probably* and *likely* in (indirect) directives. Examples are:

- Attendance at staff meetings probably amounts to 14 hours in the year; attendance at the Board of the Faculty perhaps 6–10 hours; attendance at the Improvements Committee and course sub-committees perhaps 30–40 hours.

- Consultations with colleagues and students about a current subject should probably appear under B: Associated Work.

- Other – every subject is likely to require at least 40 hours per semester for this.

- the total of A + B + C + D should probably fall between 1800 and 2400.

Again, at a rather general level the function of *perhaps*, *probably* and *likely* can be said to modalize the expression of directive meaning and to that extent these items appear in this context to be candidates for classification as components of the discourse of solidarity. However, the factors which govern their distribution appear to be somewhat different from and somewhat more specific than those operating at the general level of discourse. It is not so much that solidarity meanings interface here with authority-related meanings. Rather, the writer appears to wish to allow for a considerable degree of variation in the way that individual addressees comply with these directives, because of the nature of the actions specified. Once more, it is a very specific factor which governs the expression of directive meaning – a point which is difficult to generalize and integrate into the discourse model.

A final illustration of the point is provided by the ambiguity of the modal *should* in the sentence *the course convener should allocate the 13 (or 26 or . . .) hours of lectures and inform the people involved.* Again the modalizing function of this item makes it a candidate for the discourse of solidarity. This possibility is reinforced by a certain ambiguity associated with it, since, as noted above in the discussion of *need*, ambiguity in the area of modality typically occurs in the discourse model as an exponent of the tension between interacting discourses. For example, if one were to say to a student *you should discuss this with the Head of Department*, there is a certain ambiguity (or mystification) over the precise nature of the requirement that the addressee see the Head of Department – does it derive from the speaker, from the addressee, or from some outside factor? This kind of ambiguity mystifies the question of what kind of speech act has been produced – is it a directive (with the requirement deriving from the speaker) or a statement? – an ambiguity which is typically exploited in situations where the social relationship between speaker and addressee makes it desirable to obscure directive intent. However, the interesting point about the example here is that, although it is characterized by precisely this kind of ambiguity, there is a rather different factor at work from the one just described. The sentence clearly allows both the directive reading 'I require that course conveners allocate . . .' and the statement reading 'There is a general requirement/expectation that course conveners will allocate . . .' and it may be that the reason for selecting an item which allows for this ambiguity derives in part from the general complexities of the speaker/addressee relationship discussed earlier. A far more important consideration, however, is surely the complex nature of the addressee in this case. The memorandum is addressed to all members of the Department, some of whom are course conveners (for them the directive reading is the appropriate one), some of whom are not (the statement reading is relevant to them). This then provides another illustration of the very complex interplay of general and specific factors operating in the selection of a particular linguistic form. It is extremely difficult to see how this kind of observation is compatible with a model which seeks to identify rather broad clusters of features, each identifiable as the exponent of a specific discourse, and each tied to a relatively homogeneous ideology.

There is a useful parallel to be drawn, in conclusion, between the concept of discourse as discussed here and the concept of dialect in traditional sociolinguistic studies. The concept of a regional or social dialect (more specifically, a regional or social accent) is based on the intuitively appealing assumption that the use of a particular phonological variant, $[x_1]$, is highly correlated with the use of a set of phonological variants $[x_2], [x_3] \ldots [x_n]$. A particularly clear example of this is provided by the Mitchell and Delbridge (1965) model of Australian English. This work postulates a variety called 'Broad Australian', in which the use of the variant $[\Lambda : \mathtt{I}]$ for the variable (ey) (the vowel of *late, day, rain* etc.) is correlated with the use of $[\mathtt{ə}: \mathtt{I}]$ for (i) (*seat, tree, mean* . . .), with $[\mathtt{ɒ}: \mathtt{I}]$ for (ay) (*light, tie, time* . . .) and so on. The concept 'discourse' postulates relationships between the elements governing textual features, such that the components of a given discourse are said to be inter-correlated in a similar way. For my argument here the important point about recent sociolinguistic work of the kind pioneered by Labov (1966) is that the dialect model has in effect been abandoned. Labovian methodology is based on the investigation of individual variables in isolation from each other. Certainly, in many cases general cross-variable relationships have been identified, especially for speakers at one end or the other of a sociolinguistic continuum. A speaker who scores a high non-standard index for one variable will usually use a high proportion of non-standard variants in other variables. Most speakers, however, tend not to situate themselves at the extremes of the continuum and for these speakers the cross-variable correlational patterns are much more complex. In many cases, moreover, it has been found that individual variables can be carriers of specific social meanings, not expressed in other variables. Cases in point include the relevance of Italian ethnicity to patterns of variation in (eh) and of Jewish ethnicity to variation in (oh) (Labov, 1966:293–308). A similarly idiosyncratic pattern was found in (ı) in Belfast by Milroy (1980:163). In these cases – and one would expect many more of them to emerge in future sociolinguistic studies – there will be little correlation with patterns in other variables. The point, then, is that the dialect model is useful at a relatively general level of analysis, in that it does account for certain broadly correlating clusters of features. At a more delicate level, however, the model breaks down because of the extremely complex range of sociological determinants of phonological variation. My argument has been that similar points apply to the discourse model. The model may well be useful at a somewhat general level but it cannot be regarded as a wholly satisfactory instrument for the fine-grained analysis of textual structure.

One question raised at the outset had to do with the relationship between discourse and genre in the model discussed here. The postulated connection between discourse and the social domain and the characterization of certain discourse categories as 'legal discourse', 'medical discourse', make it extremely difficult to see how a principled basis for the distinction between discourse and genre could be established. The preceding discussion suggests that the fundamental problem derives from the fact that neither discourse nor genre are primitives. Both can be interpreted as informal labels for various loosely-related clusters of features comprising such components as topic, purpose, setting, participants (age, gender, ethnicity . . .), message form, act sequence and so on (for detailed discussion of these and other components of communication see Saville-Troike (1982:137–67). The reason why it is so difficult to separate them can be seen as deriving from the fact that there are important components common to both and that the general correlational patterns involved are far too complex for anything remotely resembling a clear boundary to be drawn.[5] This is not to deny the possibility that there may be certain (heuristic) benefits to be drawn from the application of the discourse model to textual analysis. Such applications, however, need to recognize that there are limitations on the capability of the model in the sense that the correlations of the kind that it postulates need themselves to be investigated and that this investigation involves two dimensions – the one that relates ideology to language and the one that is concerned with intra-textual correlations between linguistic structures and processes. In the past most discussion appears to have focused on the first dimension. The second dimension, however, is in fact the one that lends itself more easily to empirical investigation and perhaps deserves to receive more attention than has been devoted to it so far.

Notes

1 A preliminary version of this paper was given at a meeting of the Linguistics Circle of Brisbane in June 1986. I am most grateful to members of the Circle for their comments. I am particularly grateful to Anna Shnukal and Anne Freadman for their comments on a later version.
2 I owe this point to Rodney Huddleston.
3 I owe this point to Peter Cryle.
4 The author of this memorandum, who has given permission for this text to be cited, is male – hence the use of masculine pronouns to refer to him.
5 This point is recognized in Kress, 1985c: 81–2. From my point of view the problem with the discussion here is that, although the relationship between a particular social institution (from which a given discourse arises) and the social occasions associated with such an institution (giving rise to genres) is recognized, no mechanism is suggested for assigning linguistic structures or processes (or components thereof) to one or another of those categories.

References

Brown, P. and Levinson, S. (1978), 'Universals in language usage', in E. N. Goody (ed.), *Questions and Politeness: Strategies in Social Interaction*, Cambridge: Cambridge University Press.
Fowler, R., Hodge, R., Kress, G., and Trew, A. (1979), *Language and Control*, London: Routledge & Kegan Paul.
Goffman, E. (1967), *Interaction Ritual: Essays on Face to Face Behaviour*, New York: Doubleday.
Huddleston, R. D. (1984), *Introduction to the Grammar of English*, Cambridge: Cambridge University Press.
Kress, G. (1985a), 'Socio-linguistic development and the mature language user: different voices for different occasions', in G. Wells and J. Nicholls (eds), *Language Learning: an interactional perspective*, Lewes: Falmer Press.
Kress, G. (1985b), 'Ideological structures in discourse', in T. A. Van Dijk (ed.), *Handbook of Discourse Analysis*, vol. 4, London: Academic.
Kress, G. (1985c), 'Discourses, texts, readers and pro-nuclear arguments', in P. Chilton (ed.), *Language and the Nuclear Arms Debate: Nukespeak Today*, London: Frances Pinter.
Kress, G. and Hodge, R. (1979), *Language as Ideology*, London: Routledge & Kegan Paul.
Labov, W. (1966), *The Social Stratification of English in New York City*, Washington, DC: Center for Applied Linguistics.
Milroy, L. (1980), *Language and Social Networks*, Oxford: Blackwell.
Mitchell, A. G. and Delbridge, A. (1965), *The Speech of Australian Adolescents*, Sydney: Angus & Robertson.
Saville-Troike, M. (1982), *The Ethnography of Communication*, Oxford: Blackwell.

SALLY STOCKBRIDGE

PROGRAMMING ROCK 'N' ROLL: THE AUSTRALIAN VERSION

The following essay is a history of the construction of conventions of music programming for youth on Australian TV. In some respects, then, it could be a history of standardization, or of the dominant national rock music programme *Countdown*, and the introduction of the now ubiquitous video music or rock clip. More than this, it is about the maintenance of, and struggle for, difference within programming and the struggle to maintain a boundary between youth culture and the mainstream. For Australians, it is also a history of cultural imperialism and local interventions.

Early Australian music programming

Popular music programming in Australia began shortly after the commencement of television itself (*c.* 1956). Television, rock and roll, and the concept of 'youth' were all coincidentally post World War II phenomena.

The history of rock music programming on Australian television is a history of cultural imperialism or straight borrowing; in this case, of both the music and the programme format. Australian TV had its first rock-and-roll show in mid-1958 on HSV 7 (Melbourne). Called *Your Hit Parade*, it reflected a 1950s practice in the area of popular music – the repetition of the same song by different artists except, in this case, all 'hits' were mimed. In the 1950s 'covers' predominated; it was the song that was sold and resold rather than the artist. The era of 'rock stars' had not yet begun. *Your Hit Parade* also reflected a general absence of Australian material. The 'hits' were mimed often by people who became Australian rock personalities in their own right but the material at this stage was mainly American. The programme was a straight copy of an American programme, even to having the same name. The US version had commenced in 1950 and lasted till 1959.

In 1958 and 1959 a practice commenced with *Bandstand* (TCN 9) and *Six O'Clock Rock* (ABC 2) that was to continue throughout sixties rock music programming: the use of visiting Australian rock/pop stars to compère programmes and the use of live acts in the studio, no longer miming, but actually performing what was often their own material; Johnny O'Keefe was the most well-known Australian promoter of this situation.

Most Australian programming at this stage was based on either British or American models. TCN 9's *Bandstand* was based on *American Bandstand* which had commenced only one year before, while the format of Johnny O'Keefe's ABC 2 *Six O'Clock Rock* was based on the British *6–5 Special*. In the 1960s programmes included interviews, audience competitions, and live studio performances, often with a pre-recorded band and live lead vocals. The format in general was Top 40. There were no film clips as such until *GTK*, though studio performances were filmed and today have the look of early performance clips.

The programme that took Australia into the 1970s was *GTK*, a Channel 2 ABC National programme produced and directed variously by Paddy Conroy, Bernard Cannon, Albie Thoms, and Stephen Maclean. It had a variable length, usually between 10 and 15 minutes, and a timeslot in the afternoon, 6.30 p.m., that placed it after *Bellbird* (a country-based soap and precursor of another – *A Country Practice*) and before the ABC news. Described as a 'filler', its placement within the stations' daily programme schedule meant that it had the potential to attract a wide age-range audience for contemporary popular music, at least 70 per cent of which was Australian. *GTK* commenced a virtual ABC monopoly in pop/rock music programming for the 1970s, something that hadn't been the case in the 1960s, and wasn't to be the case in the 1980s except in one respect: the dominance of *Countdown* over all other rock music programming.

When it commenced in 1969, *GTK* was the only rock music programme that had national coverage. The early *GTK* shows were mixtures of live performance and 'nonsense', according to Cannon. Everything was done 'on the cheap' with some very *ad hoc* arrangements with record companies in relation to visiting bands. Bernie Cannon, and others, would sometimes do a clip for an artist for about $5–600. They were produced at minimal expense with an ABC crew, sometimes in an empty ABC studio, and often in the director's own time. Clips were not a priority with record companies and live work in the studio and on location used to constitute most of the programme. Other components of the programme used interviews with Australian musicians and other performers (e.g. Barry Humphries and Germaine Greer), segments of overseas footage, and clips from the recording companies (e.g. Alice Cooper's 'Schools Out'). *GTK*'s completed format could easily compare with one of the current ½ or 1 hour rock music programmes, except that *GTK* placed a considerable emphasis on Australian material, live performance, and interviews with a range of people involved in the arts, in general, as well as with rock culture in particular. 'Variety' was a much more popular format for programmes in the 1970s than is apparent in the 1980s where wall to wall video music clips and minimal speech by compères tends to dominate.

Flashez was another ABC programme which started in mid-1976 at 4.30 p.m. moving to a later timeslot of 5.30–6.30 p.m. Monday to Friday in February 1977. Very much like the 1986 programme *Edge of the Wedge*, *Flashez* provided five different programmes for five days of the week, each with its own producer/director and each with its own emphasis. Only one of these focused upon the rock and pop scene. All programmes were targeted at a teenage audience. The *TV Times* described the Thursday programme that covered rock music, produced and directed by Ralph Montague (now ABC Perth):

> *Flashez*, the ABC-TV national daily teenage show has become the first local TV program to provide regular cover of the U.S. rock and pop scene. It has appointed former *GTK* and *Funky Road* front man Stephen Maclean as its New York correspondent. Maclean will report weekly on latest U.S. fads, fashions and industry moves, and supply interviews with leading American stars. The New York appointment is part of the new, 'heavier' version of the popular *Flashez*, which has also been moved to a later – 5.30 p.m. – timeslot in a move to catch a wider audience. The show will still feature rock singer Ray Burgess and Mike Meade as front men, but the emphasis will shift from teenybopper top-20 style pop to include a wider range of rock music. Executive producer George Pugh said the new-look *Flashez* would consist of about one-third musical content. The rest would be made up of specialist features, such as Sportflash, in which top sporting heroes such as cricketer Dennis Lillee, surfer Mark Warren and others would report on the state of their glamour sports. Other successful segments which will be included in the later time slot include the Dear Suzy segment, in which Sydney newspaper columnist Suzy Jarrett discusses teenage problems; record reviews; in-studio interviews with pop guests conducted by Ray Burgess; and monthly competitions with valuable prizes. (*TV Times*, 29 January 1977 : 5)

In addition to the programme itself, *Flashez* produced a magazine called *Flashez* which sold for $1, and had badges and t-shirts carrying the programme logo. *Countdown Magazine* followed a very similar though glossier format when it came out in the 1980s. Ralph Montague suggested that the programme began to rate reasonably well, a plus for the ABC since this early timeslot had not previously rated. These few video music clips included in the programme were obtained from record companies or old *GTK* footage. In 1977 record companies did not have large collections of clips; EMI, for example, had a total collection numbering fifty in that year.

These initial examples serve to indicate a number of significant aspects of the 'framing' or format of rock/pop music programming in Australia. There was a heavy reliance upon overseas patterns of organization, and *ad hoc* arrangements (e.g. GTK) were necessitated by the low priority given the content within the TV station's schedule. Programmes were contextualized as 'youth' programming rather than music programming. The emphasis was on a variety of material that would be of interest to a youthful audience with music foregrounded because 'youth' foreground it, rather than for any other reason. Rock music, television, and the teenager as an entity and a market force appear to have emerged, or been constructed, simultaneously but rock music had not at this point been provided with a specific, separate position. It is positioned as one aspect, among others, of youth culture and framed by the discourses that construct that 'culture'.

This 'variety' format, based upon representations of 'youth culture', continues to provide one of a number of possible formats for rock music programming on Australian TV. Contemporary examples include *Beatbox* (ABC 2), *Edge of the Wedge* (ABC 2), *After Dark* (7) and to a lesser degree *Rockit* (TCN 9), and *Kulture Shock* (SBS 28).

Contemporary music programming – dominant and alternative

Media entrepreneur, Phil Tripp's, 1985 report for the Australian Film Commission suggested that the acceptance of 'variety', with its relationship to the segmentalized nature of TV, was the dominant position of TV executives: In the report he stated that:

> For the past 3 years, network programs considered clip programs to be a highly risky venture with a limited audience appeal. They favoured events programming such as concert simulcasts from Australia and overseas music specials instead. But the programs are looking at overseas trends more and now planning national(?) programs that would combine clips, news and other segments that could appeal to a broad audience. (n.p.)

For all that, however, these programming ideas were not reflected in the programmes that did go to the air during the period from 1981–1985. The only programme existing prior to 1985 that had this format, *After Dark*, was axed in 1985. It was only the ABC which took up the variety format with *Beatbox* (1985), and *Edge of the Wedge* (March 1986–October 1986). To a lesser degree, *Rockit*, which lasted six months on TCN 9 in 1985, also included variety in its format but this was inclined towards youth-oriented information and activities; for example, taking a crew into venues like discos and dance clubs to show a younger audience, who were not eligible to attend, what they were like. *Kulture Shock*, which also only survived for a short length of time (1985–1986 SBS), provided variety in the form of locations and a linking story line for a group of madcap presenters, rather than fulfilling the notions of combination expressed above. In fact, the combination programming was hardly taken up; instead the networks turned to the form of programming they had previously assumed so risky, continuous music videos.

With the exception of *Solid Gold* (10), *Continental Drift* (SBS), *After Dark* (7), and *Wavelength* (9) to a lesser degree, were continuous music videos interrupted only by the compère or by advertising. In 1985 *Rockit*, *Beatbox*, and *Kulture Shock* were the exceptions with both *Continental Drift* and *Wavelength* axed and *After Dark* soon to finish. In 1986 only *Beatbox* (2) and *Edge of the Wedge* (2) survived, though tenuously, while all other twenty national and state programmes were essentially clip programmes.

Whether or not clip programmes are indeed 'risky' is questionable. They are frequently axed for other reasons, and also sometimes brought back through popular demand; for example, *Music Video*, which was axed in December 1983, was returned in November 1984. One thing the programmers did not mention to Tripp is that they are extremely cheap to produce and also provide an 'Australian' programme component for the station, that is, material considered to be an Australian product. It could be that the general aesthetic conservatism of TV institutions has more to do with the construction of network discourses on music programming than with specific notions of risk (Ellis, 1982 : 211).

It is necessary to divide up the programmes themselves in order to ascertain their degree of risk-taking and in order to determine the dominant forms of programming and the nature of the alternatives that are presented. It is not so much the inclusion of clips that determines risk but the inclusion of particular kinds of clips, the nature of the commentary on them, and the nature of the other inclusions and exclusions: framing and programming.

Most TV programming appears to follow conventional formulae and music video programmes are no exception. What is of interest here is the fact that some programmes do step outside their formula, and the ways in which this is done. Contemporary Australian programmes could be divided as follows into those that follow(ed) a conventional formula and those that seek various alternatives, or provide various resistances, to the 'standard':

Conventional	*Alternative*
Music Video (10 Syd&Melb)	Rockit (9 Syd&Melb)
Saturday Jukebox (BTQ 7 Bris)	Nightmoves (10 all states)
Top 40 Video (SAS 10 Adel)	Wavelength (9 Network)
Sounds (7 Syd&Melb)	Night Tracks (TVT 9 Tas)
Countdown (ABC)	The Noise (SBS)
Trax (SAS 10 Adel)	Beatbox (ABC)
Seven Rock (BTQ 7 Bris)	Rock Arena (ABC)
Music Express (ADS 7 Adel)	Beat Club (SBS)
Solid Gold (10 Syd&Melb)	Edge of the Wedge (ABC)
FM TV (TVW 7 Perth)	Kulture Shock (SBS)
Simulrock (SAS 10 Adel.)	Rock around the
Clips (QTQ 9 Bris)	World (SBS)
After Dark (ATN 7 Syd)	Continental Drift (SBS)
MTV (9 Network)	Rage (ABC)
Between the Teeth (ABC)	

The 'alternatives' must be divided further in order to discuss the nature of their alternative status. The heavy reliance on overseas programming practices and the radio format provide the launching pad for a discussion of the conventions of Australian contemporary TV music video programming.

Chief amongst the conventional programmes in Australia (up until mid-1987) was *Countdown*. *Countdown* was on ABC TV and was a national programme televized every Sunday from 6–7 p.m. or 5–6 p.m. if you live in Western Australia. It was also significant for its access to country viewers, who, until recently, had few or no viewing options apart from ABC TV. It was therefore the closest programme we had to the market position occupied by *MTV* (24-hour cable TV) in the USA. This is a point to be returned to in relation to both the conventions and assumed effects of video music clip programming. The US programme *MTV* commenced in 1981, seven years after *Countdown*. But while *Countdown* had established standard practices of its own it was considerably affected by the practices of the cable programming format.

> The video clip is only part of the material broadcast in the 'Vee-jay' format of *MTV*. Approximately 10–12 clips per hour alternate with direct address by the Vee-jay, who also delivers 'news' or details about stars, clips or tours, presented with a news 'window' and interviews as if it were a regular news broadcast. Sports casts are also mimicked with a 'scoreboard'-like look of tour dates, as well as the 'Friday Night Video Fights', which are actually polls in which viewers can call in to select one of two clips as favourite. The *MTV* animated logo, plus trailers for coming attractions are also aired in rotation, along with advertisements with the 'high tech' look of the video clips: many of these ads are hard to distinguish from rock video clips; whether ad or clip remains in doubt until either the 'label' of the singer, song and album is superimposed and the name of a product is given. . . . There are also a significant number of 'interactive' advertisements where viewers call in orders for a product to a telephone number on screen, along with contests promoted by **MTV** in which the viewers mail in their names. . . . Plus, there are other 'interactive' gimmicks, for example, a pseudo-pirate of the airwaves, who 'interferes' with *MTV* programming. . . . This non-rock video material can vary in a ratio from 1:1 to 1:2 with the actual rock music programming, depending on the length of the clips, the number of ads and the choice of the programs. (Morse, 1985:166–7)

In 1987 *Countdown* opened with, and continued to present itself as, 'pirate TV'. In its own search for difference, *Countdown* mimicked *MTV*. This didn't last very long though. Within the space of no more than two months *Countdown* had reverted to something close to its previous format (and in July 1987 was axed – another story). *Countdown*'s similarity to *MTV* also lay in its ability to command certain exclusivity rights over the screening of music videos. Its compère, Ian 'Molly' Meldrum, was suggested to hold the record companies in thrall. If he didn't obtain 'first cab off the rank' status with a band and video, it was unlikely that they would be given another chance on *Countdown* unless popularity was so high he could not afford to exclude them.

But Molly paid nothing for clips, pay-for-play had not been instigated. *Countdown* was vital to record companies because it commanded the highest TV audience rating – partly because the viewers knew that the bands/videos would be there first – a circular rationale. *Countdown* commenced in the Melbourne studios of the ABC in November 1974. This had immediate implications for *Flashez*. The budget was cut and restrictions were placed in the number of pop clips that could be played and even before this they had to be cleared with *Countdown* first. According to Montague, pressure was brought to bear by the executive producer of *Countdown* to the disadvantage of the Sydney programme. Montague saw *Flashez* as an alternative form of youth programming because of its varied information based content, focused on what was assumed to be relevant to that age group. What was of 'relevance' was determined by the producers and corresponded to the inflow of music and fashion from the USA and Great Britain.

Countdown occupied prime child-viewing time and rated well enough to be repeated within the same week. Significantly, it qualified as both Australian and children's content or programming. The position that *Countdown* occupied in relation to the record companies and therefore also in relation to other music programmes allowed it the power to determine and alter the standards and conventions of this kind of programming. This situation, I would argue, still holds in spite of its demise on 19 July 1987. *Countdown* included: Top 40 singles; interviews with bands; video music clips; live studio performance; Molly's commentary – 'Humdrum' – providing information on his favourites, tour dates, present and future high achievers; UK Top 5 singles, US Top 5; Australian Top 5; National Top 10; Chartbusters.

There are two slightly different definitions of 'standard'. The first refers to regularity and uniformity, an example of which is the notion of 'broadcast quality'. If a video music clip is to gain air time it must conform to these standards. It must be on 1-inch tape and the sound and visual quality must match up to the minimum required by that TV station. The second meaning refers to the construction of degrees of excellence. But as Bordwell, Staiger, and Thompson (1985:96) argued in relation to the film industry,

> The standardization process must be thought of not as an inevitable progression toward dull, mediocre products but instead, particularly in competitive cases, as an attempt to achieve a precision-tooled quality object. Once established, the standard becomes a goal to be attained.

This is a very useful definition of standardization since it also allows for the changes and novelty that programmes must incorporate in order to maintain their market share. *Countdown*'s commencement date of November 1974 coincided with the advent of colour TV in Australia. The programme was chosen to advertise colour TVs in department stores. Used here as a marketing device for colour, *Countdown* itself could also be seen to be a marketing device for Top 40 singles. The early format of *Countdown* was of 'live' performances interspersed with commentary. This live performance was a result of a scarcity of overseas material. There were very few filmclips available. But the so-called 'live' performances were also constructed. The band in the studio would mime to a single mix without the lead vocal and the lead singer would sing the vocal live to the audience. Synchronized sound significantly predated the advent of video music clips. *Countdown* was originally a half hour programme produced in the Melbourne studios of the ABC. Paul Drane, an early producer/director, was the only person making film clips (shot on 16mm) for local and predominantly Melbourne bands, for example, Dragon, or AC/DC. All of those were shot on a 16mm reversal film stock and constituted only a few days' work for each clip.

The production of film clips by *Countdown* personnel was initially beneficial for the Australian bands who were included. The emphasis of the whole programme was local, by necessity. However, once overseas band clips became available the situation changed. Stephen Jones (ABC Melbourne) argues that *Countdown* started the 'convention' of bands having a video image. 'A lot of overseas acts would come out for promotional tours and wouldn't have a clip with them. They wouldn't be performing here but would have an appearance on *Countdown*. Often impressed with the speed of the clip production, some would take the clip with them to use as future promotion.' Like *MTV* in the USA, *Countdown* also argued that it placed a great deal of emphasis on the results of market research. The role of executive producers has previously been mentioned in relation to influence over other programmes in the same station but they also exercised a great deal of control over the inclusions within their own programming sphere. This included major creative decisions determining the aesthetic features of a programme.

Countdown studio designers were given the freedom to experiment with new techniques away from the standard sets. However, these changes were not simply about innovation or the desires of the market. The standard-setter must also keep ahead of the other programmes with which it is in competition. In *Countdown*'s case it had to maintain its leading position if it was also to maintain its most exceptional feature – first play of new clip singles. Thus, *Countdown* had to stand out from all the other programmes, it had to maintain its difference. (This became increasingly difficult in 1987.) Apparently, the programme went through a period in 1984 when it was felt it had outgrown itself. Most of the people working on it were ten years older and their musical tastes no longer suited the target audience upon which they were based. The target age group was still 10–17 years. While technology was utilized to 'maintain difference' the original target group and format of Top 40 clips was adhered to. Thus, Grant Rule, executive producer, explained: 'It's what the ABC decided on specifically for the viewing of a young age group and we have to follow that brief. But we are open for unique clips if they are presented' (*Encore*, 19 July–1 August 1984: VI). Executive producers had a longer association and therefore greater control over the programme. Producers apparently experienced a high turnover. Grant Rule oversaw all popular music programming on the ABC; other programmes of which he is and was executive producer are *Rock Arena* and *Between the Teeth*.

Controversy over local content began in the 1980s, coinciding with the introduction of clips supplanting live performance. Even though local content could also be seen to fit into Rule's definition of 'unique clips', the Top 40 format and the demand for certain 'standards' led to the exclusion of a lot of Australian material. The rationale for this was all couched within terms of 'quality'. Jon Kennett, clip production co-ordinator, of RCA:

> I used to be the number one Molly (Ian Meldrum) knocker, but looking at programming of television like radio, songs have to be selected in terms of

quality. Putting out lower budget clips or recordings against overseas material – especially higher budget product from the US and the UK – and it makes sense for a program to go for the flashier and higher quality clips in order to maintain appeal and ratings. You can't apportion that blame on Molly or the program. (*Encore*, 19 July–1 August 1984: VI)

But Molly actively played the role of 'bard' (Fiske and Hartley, 1980). To be included on *Countdown* gave a band credibility as far as the industry and the young viewers of the programme were concerned. The band/artist was rendered significant and most bands/artists acknowledged the operation of this process by the efforts they went to in order to obtain a screening. However, it is normal practice for a record company to approach the TV programme producers, not for the band or band manager to do it themselves. Record companies, in the main, believed in *Countdown*.

> *Countdown* is part of our marketing mix, a major part of our promotions. It's very important, I'd hate it not to exist. Molly is respected world wide. I have only to send a telex saying Molly is coming and the place starts jumping. He knows everyone in the industry round the world and everyone knows him. (*National Times*, 9–15 November 1984: 29)

As talent co-ordinator, Molly was the arbiter of quality. *Countdown*'s and Molly's own sheer longevity increased their perceived legitimacy (*Metro*, 64, 1984: 39). (But it didn't stop them from being axed. Even the standard bearers are subject to change.) Meldrum, executive producer Grant Rule, and two producers met every Tuesday to decide on the content of the programme. 'The music chosen is not left or right or extremist but contemporary', according to Rule. 'We keep our music selection fresh there's no reason why we can't last another ten years. We're sitting very well in the market because of the national network' (*Metro*, 64, 1984: 39).

The dominant conventions can be detected within these industry statements, conventions governed by the priority placed upon a certain target audience and upon the inclusion of video music clips. These priorities also led to lobbying and political pressures within the management of the ABC securing these interests for *Countdown* and placing other programming in jeopardy. *GTK* and *Flashez*, both Sydney programmes, lost ground to *Countdown*. Later other programmes would also be affected, not only those on the ABC.

There was little change in the *Countdown* format from 1984 to 1985. In 1986, however, computer graphics were introduced in the programme logo with Chromakey and other graphics throughout the programme, the introduction and signature tune were changed, and all sections within the programmes were shortened to a new, rather clipped style. Previously, small snippets of clips and songs were included in the charts, i.e. Top 5, Chartbusters etc.; in 1986 only the titles and one still from the clip were included. The snappier promotional format altered a previously more relaxed format that appeared to be based more on Molly's chatty, rambling presence than on the needs of advertising. The 1986 format appeared to foreground the links between the programme and its function as promotion. From the 1970s to the 1980s *Countdown* changed from predominantly live performances in the studio to the playing of video clips. As a result, Australian material gave way to overseas material. This leads to the issue of exclusion. Framing processes include exclusion as the other side of inclusion. It is rarely apparent except to those who have been affected by the process. Practices of exclusion operate to establish the boundaries of legitimacy within a particular system or discursive formation. Those excluded do not fulfil or do not wish to fulfil the criteria for inclusion. In the case of *Countdown* bands/artists were excluded, against their will, because they did not reach the 'standards' set. Some bands (e.g. Midnight Oil) excluded themselves because they did not wish to be seen to fulfil those criteria. The definitions they provided for themselves are at a variance with the definitions incorporated by the programme. In the case of *Countdown* these were as stated – Top 40, mainstream, commercial, directed towards 10–17-year-olds, usually signed under a large record company, broadcast quality video clip, G-rated, 'non-extremist'.

The practices of exclusion of such mainstream programmes is similar to the US. The policy of *MTV* is to target an audience whose norm is 'white suburban and male'. Black bands in the USA find it difficult to get a clip screened on *MTV* unless they are 'socially acceptable' 'cross-over' examples, like, of course, Michael Jackson, or Lionel Richie. There has been an extensive network of alternative broadcasting developed that caters for so-called non-crossovers (Hoberman, 1983:36).

The main exclusions from programmes that are specifically top 40 in orientation are bands/artists who can be described as 'independent'. Though independent can mean a number of things, independent frequently implies poor financing and a lack of a record company contract. For bands/artists in this category inclusion on *Countdown* or similar programmes is almost a total impossibility. Not only must they meet the cost of a sound recording of their music to a standard acceptable on such broadcast TV programmes, but also the increasingly high cost of a video clip which also must be up to standard. Of course, even after a clip has been produced it may not be screened. If the band is signed to a record company the company may in future be unwilling to make a video clip, since they pay the initial costs. Even if the clip never goes to air the cost of production eventually comes out of the royalties payable to the band. Both record company and band lose, but the band loses more. *Countdown*'s attitude to Australian bands has been criticized since 1984 in the industry magazine, *Encore* (*Encore*, music Video supplement, 1984: VI).

> Look at the past year and you will see a drop in Australian clips that is terrible for both artists and record companies. Overseas clips occupy the majority of time on *Countdown* and Australian artists are lucky to get on which is especially disappointing as that program was one of the biggest influences in the growth of Australian Music. (Michael Gudinski, Mushroom Records)

There's not as much support for local acts as there should be with new bands asked to perform live rather than having their clips shown negating investment we make in clips aimed at the program and its audience. (Michael Mathews, EMI)

The situation for 1985 and 1986 was not significantly different. A breakdown by segment of a couple of programmes demonstrates that the majority of clips screened were of overseas artists and live acts were usually Australian. However, if overseas acts were touring they would be given a live spot on *Countdown*. Whatever the case, the number of live acts in relation to clips was significantly reduced. The emphasis on overseas acts was maintained. Thus, independent here can mean with record company contract or it can mean without. It can also mean non-mainstream Australian. Independent in this context may simply mean working outside of the mainstream of large record company contracts and mainstream TV programming. It does not necessarily have anything to do with the form or content of the music produced or the video clips constructed. There are also independent groups who may be considered fringe or sub-cultural. Their work can be excluded for political reasons or reasons pertaining to preconceived conventions of standards and quality. Anything 'extremist' in Grant Rule's terms would be excluded.

Alternatives – localism

As in the USA, the different Australian states have their own music programmes, for example, the Adelaide programme *Simulrock* and the Brisbane programme *Clips*. These programmes are not tightly scripted and are compèred by DJs from local FM Radio. *Simulrock* considers itself to be risk-taking with local and independent material included along with a 'classics' segment of film clips from the 1970s. The same producer, John Olszewski, controls both *Trax* and *Simulrock* but argues that late-night *Simulrock* is much more flexible than the early programme. *Simulrock* has also produced a couple of local clips, for example, Uforia's 'Miles Away'. *Simulrock*, and *FMTV* Perth, are both simulcast on local FM Radio. Like *FMTV*, *Simulrock* allows very little linking speech. While these programmes consider themselves to be risk-taking they maintain a format very similar to the US's *MTV* and their only 'alternative' feature is the inclusion of some local video clips. What is absent from all these programmes is live performance and any acknowledgement through interview or commentary of the work of the film clip directors. These programmes approximate to a radio-programme format. They also conform to the practices of 'localism' like some US programmes. US programming includes local shows that must struggle for survival in the face of the *MTV* monolith. But while *MTV* must struggle to obtain the advertising dollar, it is localism on many fronts that keeps these programmes afloat. They receive local advertising that national networks can't get, emphasis is also on the local in their music programming. They focus on local groups, local events, local concerts, and use local radio

DJs as their VJs. The connections between local radio outlets are tight, but they are also almost totally hit-orientated, and don't take risks on non-Top 40 material (*Billboard*, 6 October 1984: 26–8).

One thing that links all 'alternative' programmes is the active, conscious desire for difference. But difference is not conceived simply as a marketing strategy, rather the difference here resides within a consideration of the range of music available and the range of formats possible. It is not repetition but novelty that is the central focus of these examples of programming. This is not to say, however, that some repetition does not exist within the programmes and across all programmes or that the producers were not interested in ratings. What has been considered to date are processes of standardization, conventional practices, and dominant methods of programming. What is of interest in the following programmes is their possible status as 'alternatives', not from outside but from *within* what can be conceived of as the dominant apparatus of broadcast television.

On TCN 9's *Wavelength*, the ubiquitous presenter, Jonathon Coleman, utilized a particular formula which attempted to parody or subvert the clips he screened. Jono would chroma-key himself into the clip with the deliberate intention of altering the unconsciously serious nature of programmes like *Countdown*. His form of comedy was not appreciated by the most serious of youthful viewers, however, though he and Dano (Ian Rogerson) are popular radio presenters on Sydney's 2MMM-FM. His approach wasn't appreciated by Channel 9 producers, either, who axed the programme after only one year. At the time, however, it was considered quite viable. *Wavelength* was the only national daily afternoon music video programme and after initial doubts as to its viability, it had mainstreamed ratings and increased viewership in its time slot. The programme apparently rated well in Perth, Victoria, and NSW. *Wavelength* incorporated an altered role for the compère, who no longer played the bard, but was a satirist and subverter of mainstream music. Coleman believed that US clips especially were too glossy and boring and could easily have been re-cut to make shampoo commercials! Coleman initially had a free rein on *Wavelength* but he and Rogerson had many arguments with the programme's producer who, as an ex-9 employee, was concerned about what was appropriate for the television station. The first 6–7 months included a lot of experimentation which was gradually dropped as pressures were brought to bear. *Wavelength* also had to delay screening clips until *Countdown* had screened its preferences. For at least some of its existence, then, *Wavelength* included an altered format with Jono interrupting clips rather than linking them.

Rockit went to air at the same time as *Sounds* but did not wish to compete with the more established programme. Rather, it sought to establish a different audience, some of whom may have watched the earlier late-night programme, *Nightmoves*. Unlike many other compères, and though he had a radio background, Lee Simon was not simply a front person. Like Molly Meldrum and Donny Sutherland (Sounds) he was also heavily involved in the content. Inasmuch as he played the role of bard and conceived of TV programming in similar terms to that of radio programming *Rockit* was conventional. Simon also approached the programme within a context of localism including segments shot in local venues. What was different here, though, relates both to format and content. The comic duo, Los Trios Ringbarkus, were introduced as 'spoof' market researchers breaking down, like *Wavelength*, the 'serious' conventions of rock music programming. The stated emphasis on alternative bands and independently produced videos was carried through as was a programming preference for Australian material. However, instead of end-to-end clips by different artists, *Rockit*, named after Herbie Hancock's single of the same name, included longer specials on bands (such as The Models), and on music clip-makers. Clip-makers from Australia and overseas were interviewed with examples of their work for different bands. The creative input of all participants was always acknowledged. The programme emphasized video sales and releases as well as singles and albums and didn't repeat previously screened material. Most mainstream programmes repeat top rating video clips or put them into 'rotation'. On *Rockit* they were screened once only. The programme was produced by Wired Productions which again links it back to Michael Gudinski at Mushroom Records, rather than the 9 Network.

Kulture Shock had an experimental and somewhat off-beat alternative format. It included lesser known band clips and live (pre-recorded) performances often taken from *The Tube* and other programmes from Europe that were bought by SBS. *Rock Around The World* was the first SBS rock music programme to do so and its replacement, *Kulture Shock*, continued the practice. *Kulture Shock* based much of its subversion of conventional standards on Channel 4's *The Tube* and represented a struggle on the part of exec-producer Wayne Simpson to devise a different format for rock music programming. This programme wasn't continued after the first year, neither were *Wavelength* or *Rockit*, and Simpson went on to maintain the role of exec-producer of *The Noise*, SBS, but not to maintain the struggle over format.

Wavelength and *Kulture Shock* both emphasized difference rather than 'flow' (Williams, 1974). Disjunction and interruption were utilized as alternative practices within the programme. In the case of *Rockit* it was often the independently produced clips that produced this effect. For example, the video music clip produced by Philip Brophy in Melbourne for Olympic Sideburns 'I Travel' was screened during the second edition of *Rockit*. It was shot on video tape to intentionally stand out from, to disrupt, the flow of clips shot on 16mm and 35mm film stock. The approach of some clip-makers is to produce this effect as an oppositional device; others, of course, use it as a device in order to simply be noticed amongst all the others. But it is still the discrete unit that is sought, rather than flow.

These units can be packaged or framed in different ways. Most programmes include clips as individual units named by the band and the single, other programmes link a group of clips together linked by the band and album, although probably all directed by different clip-makers. It is only in some alternative programming that groups of clips may be linked in a segment together under the name of the clip-maker who directed them all.

Rockit and *Rock Arena* are the only Australian programmes that have done so. These linking devices are indicative of different organizational practices, and they introduce the possibility of competing voices. Programme(r)s that only link band/artist to music video clip eliminate some of the competition and, therefore, the contradictions that may be present between the music and the visuals, for example, let alone between the personnel involved in each different area. What is of interest here is the way some programmes include these different and potentially contradictory levels and others don't. The latter provide a simplified picture, the former one of greater complexity. Different contexts then, provide different viewing possibilities and different meanings. Organization or programming can confer different meanings on the material it includes partly due to the way in which it is included.

Beatbox was particularly interesting in this regard since it was the most overt organizer of material and the only prescriptive programme in relation to youth culture. Like *Edge of the Wedge* it was a 'variety' programme but it sought to influence as well as to inform, making use of video music clips rather than simply screening them. *Beatbox* was simulcast on Sydney's 2JJJ-FM though it went to air nationally. Here video music clips were inserted within the framing device of various themes perceived to be relevant to the assumed 10–25-year-old audience of the generally working-class, western suburbs. As with *Kulture Shock*, the point of insertion would tend to lend specific meanings to the clip selected emphasizing it's ability to somehow illustrate the theme chosen. Examples of themes included: relationships, teenage motherhood, racism, tattoos, head banging, rebels vs. conservative school kids, etc. Musicians were sometimes interviewed themselves in relation to the theme, e.g. Angry Anderson of Rose Tattoo on tattoos. Viewers were invited to participate in the programme also, by being interviewed in relation to a theme, or by viewing a film for which tickets were provided and then assessing it. Hence music was not foregrounded, as it is in other contemporary programmes, but contextualized, as in the earlier *Flashez*, as one important part of youth culture in general.

Beatbox was partly funded by a $230,000 grant from the Department of Employment and Industrial Relations' Community Employment Program and was centred on and produced by young people from Sydney's western suburbs. The programme was prescriptive though progressive in its politics and was organized in a conscious manner, rather than presumed 'natural'. The 'framing' within the programme was overt and deliberate, rather than covert and determined by discourses of 'quality' and 'popularity' (*Sun Herald*, 19 May 1985 : 51). *Beatbox* was axed in June 1987 because of stated funding cuts but by July 1987 the managing director of the ABC, David Hill, suggested it would return as soon as funds were available, perhaps within two months (*Sydney Morning Herald*, The Guide, 13–19 July 1987). *The Factory* has now replaced it (and *Countdown*).

Rock Arena commenced in 1980 in Perth. It was originally intended to include live performances and old footage of, for example, Cat Stevens, Beatles, Joan Armatrading etc. All material was obtained from record company archives which had never been tapped before. The programme was a flexible length since it was the last programme at night. It was partly nostalgic and partly composed of concerts shot by the ABC crew, and interviews. There was no specific emphasis except that video music clips were not included. The programme was produced by two staff members, Ian Parmenter and Peter Holland, in one day and was cheap, low-priority television. This situation changed when the programme was taken over by Melbourne ABC and placed in the *Countdown* stable. Funds that had not previously been provided were now available along with most of the *Countdown* crew. The compère, Suzanne Dowling, came from 2JJJ-FM in Sydney, bringing with her a preference for independent bands, clips, and clip-makers. To a large degree *Rock Arena* represents in format and content those aspects that *Countdown* excluded. It is researched in great detail and provides an even mix of independent Australian and non-mainstream overseas bands. Dowling's role, like Basia, must be described as 'fact'-providing but it is not judgemental in the way Donnie, Molly and Annette, etc. were. The programme includes specials on bands, past and present independents and oppositional, and interviews with Australian clip-makers. What *Rock Arena*, *The Noise*, *Beat Box*, *Beat Club*, *Kulture Shock*, and *Rock Around the World* have in common is that none of these programmes are/were based on repetition (rotation) or promotion, or not as their chief concern. It is/was the creative and independent aspects of contemporary music that they focus on rather than the commercial. In this case they 'resist' the standardized practices of the conventional programmes and operate as alternative discursive parameters, setting in place a boundary between independence and Top 40 commodified forms and format. It is, perhaps, significant that all of these programmes are/were on the ABC and SBS, both government-sponsored non-commercial stations which broadcast nationally. (This is not, however, the sole determining factor since *Countdown* was also an ABC production, as were the *Countdown Awards*.)

It is, however, true to say that there is, in general, a greater degree of diversity in Australian music programme formats than American and that alternatives, opposition, and differences may be expressed in a variety of ways through deliberate and accidental contradiction in television programming. The sobering fact, however, is that they tend to be shortlived. There may be in Australia a greater possibility for the inclusion of the 'independent' or 'amateur' (artist and clip-maker), especially at the local level, but the dominant format still comes from overseas, along with the majority of musical material. Most record companies have their bases in the USA and the US cabler *MTV* is still the most significant yardstick of style and 'quality' in video music clips. The Australian *MTV* mimics the US *MTV* in format as do *FMTV*, *Simulrock* and other local state programmes in spite of their openness to local material. Local interventions are minimal in the face of the influx of material from overseas and the power of the record and television institutions as arbiters of 'quality'.

References

Ellis, John (1982), *Visible Fictions*, London: Routledge & Kegan Paul.

Morse, Margaret (1985), 'Rock video: synchronising rock music and TV', *Fabula*.

Bordwell, David, Staiger, Janet, and Thompson, Kristin (1985), *The Classical Hollywood Cinema*, New York: Columbia University Press.

Fiske, John, and Hartley, John (1980), *Reading Television*, London: Methuen.

Hoberman, John (1983), 'Video radio', *Film Comment*, 19, 4.

Tripp, Phil (1985), *Australian Film Commission Report on Music Video*, unpublished.

Williams, Raymond (1974), *Television, Technology and Cultural Form*, Glasgow: Fontana.

KERRY CARRINGTON

GIRLS AND GRAFFITI

My sense that graffiting is a gendered cultural practice first arose during discussions with high-school students. I interviewed a group of boys separately from a group of girls during school hours about what graffiti meant to them and whether they participated in its production. The school was chosen because its constituency included a high proportion of working-class and Aboriginal children; the assumption underlying the choice of topic was that graffiti holds a special meaning for working-class kids as an art form of the dispossessed. It gives expression to their lives in a way that 'legitimate' communication codes do not.

There was a common understanding among the boys from this school that the type of graffiti meaningful to their social relationships is what I have called rap graffiti. For a boy to consider rap graffiti meaningful he did not have to actually participate in its production. He merely had to be an audience to it and an admirer of it. All the boys interviewed had 'tag' names and regularly practised 'tagging up', although only one boy claimed to be a skilled 'bomber'. A 'tag' is a metaphor for a signature which identifies the artist's street name (see Figure A for an example). 'Bombers' plan and paint 'pieces', usually in groups of two or more. 'Pieces' are stylized, multi-colour murals, executed with spray paint, which usually depict a mammoth version of the artist's street name or insignia. 'Piece' is short for masterpiece (see Figure A for an example).

A couple of the girls interviewed from the same school expressed a desire to learn how to 'bomb' and claimed to use 'tag' names occasionally. However rap graffiti was considered a 'boy thing' and none of the girls had been involved in a planned 'bombing'. Instead the girls claimed authorship of personal inscriptions about who they love, who they hate, and who their friends are. All of the girls had been involved at one time or another in the production of the romantic and personal graffiti commonly found inscribed on toilet walls, desks and chairs. Girls' graffiti was also found on more personal items such as rubbers, rulers, books, school bags and their own bodies, particularly on their hands and arms. Girls' graffiti is not confined to the toilet wall, but it is the female toilet which plays host to the largest proportion of it.

There is no masculine equivalent to this type of graffiti. The possibility of boys writing about who they love, who they hate, and who their friends are

Figure A

on either their bodies or toilet walls should not be ruled out entirely. The point is, however, that even if boys were to participate in this sort of graffiting they would not attach any significant social meaning to it. For them, rap graffiti was the kind most meaningful to their social identity as working-class boys.

One initial difficulty with the project was how to generalize from the experience of the small sample of girls interviewed. In order to assess the assumption that toilet graffiti is in some way meaningful to working-class girls I needed to combine the interviews with other research techniques. I therefore conducted an observational study of female toilets at railway stations over a period of a year. The observations required small amounts of time, before and after school hours, or on Friday and Saturday nights, travelling on trains and hanging around platform female public toilets and taking photographs of graffiti within these toilets. Some extra time was spent during the May and August school holidays making observations of almost every station on Sydney's Western line as far as Penrith, on the Southern line as far as Cabramatta, and the Illawarra line as far as Temple.[1] Weekly recordings of new additions or changes to the toilet graffiti at Stanmore railway station[2] were made over a twelve-month period so that I could record both change and continuity.

Approximately 420 of the 492 photographs of graffiti were taken from female toilets in predominantly working-class neighbourhoods. Most of these were collected from railway stations, shopping centres, and parks. For comparative purposes a small selection of toilet graffiti from a middle-class environment and an older age group was taken from two of Sydney's three university campuses. The remaining 60 of these 420 photographs were from public female toilets in rural areas of New South Wales as far west as Bourke. In addition, another 72 photographs have been taken of rap graffiti. Most of these were found on railway property in Sydney's western and inner western suburbs. The entire collection of photographs was taken over a period of eighteen months.

Methodologically, the deployment of photographic images in the text is problematic. Photographs do not represent an unbiased reality. The power of inclusion and exclusion makes the photograph an interpretation of reality and not an irrefutable image of it (Sontag, 1977). As an image, the photograph is a created structure of meaning (Berger, 1972) which belongs to the realm of the coded, of the sign system, of language (Bergala, 1984 : 108). The interests of the photographer, the political purpose of the photograph, and its relationship to an audience are crucial considerations when using the photograph as a research instrument. The photographs contained in this text have been taken in order to assess the function of graffiti as a communication code of working-class children.

The discussion is in three parts. The first explains why the public female toilet embodies spatial relations of social significance for working-class girls. The second and third explain how power relations of cultural and economic inequality are negotiated at the micro-level of the female public toilet.

One could easily assume that toilets are places for simply relieving bodily needs which are necessary, mundane, repetitive, often stigmatized as 'dirty', and over which we are powerless. The toilet is private, personal, and trivial. Yet the stubbed cigarette butts, discarded hypodermic needles and blood stained tissues, sounds of giggling, gossip, and whispered secrets, and the myriads of graffiti, suggest that female public toilets serve needs more social than biological.

The argument is best illustrated with an example. The graffiti, 'SORRY BOYS BUT THIS IS A PRIVATE GRAFFITI ROOM XXX 000', 'NEW-INGTON FREE ZONE',[3] was taken at Stanmore Railway Station. It appears on the exterior side of the entrance door to the female toilets. What is important about this graffiti is that it defines the space as both female and social. The meaning of this toilet as a vessel for biological wastes has been subverted. It is not a toilet but a private graffiti room for girls only. Although this is not immediately apparent, the space has also been defined as class-specific through the words 'NEWINGTON FREE ZONE'. Newington is a middle-class private boys' school in Petersham. Many boys from this school get on and off their train to and from school at Stanmore railway station and are rumoured to give the local girls a 'hard time'. The fact that these same girls have expressed their preference for local working-class boys in other pieces of graffiti (e.g., 'MARRICKVILLE GUYS AND GIRLS RULE', 'STANMORE BOYS ARE THE BEST') can be interpreted to mean that Newington boys are not welcomed primarily because of their class and not because of their gender.

Middle-class girls from private girls' schools are also subject to vilification: 'ASCHRAM (sic) GIRLS STINK'. But so are girls from other localities, particularly the western suburbs. The important difference is that

Ascham girls did not respond to graffiti denigrating them, whereas it was evident in the volumes of graffiti between warring groups of working-class girls that there had been contestation over who 'ruled' the Stanmore toilets. Various groupings of girls divided by locality and ethnicity staked their claims: 'ALL PETERSHAM GIRLS ARE SLUTS'; 'MARRICKVILLE GIRLS HIGH RULES'; 'PISS OFF WESTIES THESE LOOS ARE TAKEN'; 'PETERSHAM GIRLS HIGH SCHOOL ARE THE BEST'; 'SARAH IS A SPANISH SHIT'; 'ITALIANS RULE'; 'ALL WOGS ARE FUCKED', etc. These girls are staking out the public toilet as part of their social territory, however meagre, and the graffiti in this space has become a repository for their everyday expression of lived class, gender and cultural relations. In the process the dominant meaning of the public toilet as a place for relieving body needs has been transformed.

The reason why it is the toilet and not some other social space which is being claimed and contested as social territory between warring groups of girls is complex. It is partly explained by the social relations of spatial structure. Most public spaces are not 'public' at all. Certainly the platform at Stanmore railway station is 'ruled' by Newington boys on school days before and after school hours, by railway personnel at other times, and is occasionally contested by 'bombers' and railway police late on Friday and Saturday nights. Predominantly it is boys and men who fight for control of 'public' spaces such as railway platforms. It is therefore understandable that local girls hanging out at Stanmore railway station, waiting for a train, meeting a friend, or just filling in time, find the retreat the toilet offers from Newington boys an inviting one.

For girls, the social relations of 'public' space are not the only dimension involved in their retreat to the public toilet. The attempted regulation of girls' social behaviour is in itself a major factor. Gender relations in the private space of the family also play a role. It has been well documented that girls, more than boys, are prohibited by their parents from participating in street games and other highly public leisure activities. These include hanging around shop corners, outside cinemas, and skating rinks (McRobbie, 1978a; McRobbie and Nava, 1984; Thomas, 1980; Lees, 1986; Cowie and Lees, 1983; Boys, et al., 1984; Otto, 1982). Both McRobbie (1978) and Cowie et al. (1983) argue quite explicitly that the street is a socially taboo space for girls and propose this as the reason why girls centre their leisure activities in the private space of their bedrooms. But girls' social and leisure activities do occur in public spaces such as pubs, schools, shopping centres, workplaces, and railway stations. The toilet is one place within public spaces where girls can be 'public' but 'invisible', that is, avoid the surveillance their social behaviour normally attracts, even if only for a moment to have a smoke.

What precipitates these sets of unequal social relations between girls and boys and girls and their parents is the structuring of spatial arrangements. The design, use, and control of 'public' space both expresses and gives shape to relations of domination and subordination (Castells, 1975). Space is socially produced and for this reason is not politically neutral (Amsden, 1979 : 13). Predictably, the applied research of feminist geographers has found that many 'public' spaces have been appropriated and designed with little regard to women (Women and Geography Study Group, 1984; Boys *et al.*, 1984). There is no 'Stanmore Girls Club' which offers unrestricted access and a self-determining environment, free from both boys and parental surveillance, in the same way as the Stanmore railway station does. The point is that the female toilet would not need to exist to fulfil girls' unfulfilled leisure needs if girls had equal and self-determining access to alternative leisure facilities and social resources.

The public female toilet embodies fundamental contradictions, however. External power relations define the space as a measure of girls' unequal control over public spaces, yet some girls are territorial about toilets and obviously attach some social significance to them. On the one hand they symbolize powerlessness; yet the attraction of the public toilet as a social space for girls lies in its potential as a space apparently free from boys, free from surveillance, and free from particular classes of boys – as a 'NEWINGTON FREE ZONE'. This 'freedom' is, however, a fickle one. Authority relations constituted by broader sets of cultural and economic inequality are particularly evident in two key respects. One is inscribed in spatial structure and the other in social meanings.

I have chosen the example of the New South Wales State Railway Authority (SRA) to illustrate how the spatial structure of the female public toilet embodies power relations which at first glance appear natural and neutral. Graffiti is in no way confined to SRA toilets, buildings and rolling stock, but Sydney's railways are important to its dispossessed kids as a free means of transport, an appropriate meeting place and an exciting place to hang around. Fare evasion and jumping the tracks are widespread, and are commonly practised by both girls and boys. A recent state government report identified fare evasion as a common method by which Sydney's population of 'at risk' girls protected their pitiful incomes (Women's Co-ordination Unit, 1986 : 75). The trains give these kids a mobility and a meeting place which they would otherwise be denied if they had to pay for it. The discussion below analyses how the SRA exerts its authority over the use of railway station toilets through its control of toilet technology.

The SRA employs a two-pronged strategy in the repression of graffitti. The first relies on the processes of criminalization and involves a confrontational style of authority through the use of armed patrol guards. This high profile policing has been directed mostly at boys. One day per week is set aside at Bidura Children's Court to adjudicate breaches of railway regulations by juveniles. Staffing of the Transport Investigation Branch (TIB) of the SRA was increased by 72 per cent from 144 to 247 armed patrol guards in the 1985 financial year (SRA *Annual Report*, 1985 : 13). A transit squad of detectives was also formed in the same year to assist the existing body of patrol guards and undercover detectives (SRA *Annual Report*, 1985 : 14). They are issued with batons, handcuffs, and pistols after only four months' training and allegedly have the same powers of arrest as police (Aurban, 1986 : 9). (In February 1986, the SRA was forced to disband an entire section of this branch in response to allegations of corruption.)

The second strategy employed by the SRA in the suppression of graffiti has been a technological one, aimed at the ultimate erasure of all graffiti on railway property. An extra 100 cleaners were hired in the 1985 financial year with the aim of removing graffiti from the railway's rolling stock virtually immediately (SRA *Annual Report*, 1985 : 40). In the same year graffiti removal cost $225,000 and consumed 22,700 hours of cleaning (Wilson and Healy, 1986 : 5). This strategy has been a costly and dismal failure as a deterrent to rap graffitists, its target group. Instead, the technological strategy has had a far greater unintended impact on the graffiting practices of girls. The following explains how and why.

The effects of these two strategies are felt by both male and female graffitists in very different ways. For boys the contestation between them and patrol guards of the SRA has been ritualized into a game. The boys interviewed recalled in great detail the adventure of hiding and being chased by patrol guards in the process of 'bombing' a 'piece' on railway property. For girls the contest is at a technological level, is more subtle and less exciting, and rarely involves confrontation.

Authority relations between girls and the SRA are negotiated in spatial arrangements. Several graffiti-resistant toilets were found on the Western line at Liverpool, Cabramatta, and Guildford, for instance. The striking feature of these toilets was their almost total absence of graffiti and the stark unfriendliness of the toilet atmosphere, as if they were uninhabitable, never used. The paint is non-absorbent; other surfaces were laminexed, making the removal of texta and pen inscriptions relatively easy, while the walls were constructed from an indent-proof material like patchwork concrete. The foyer to the women's toilet at Liverpool station had been appropriated by a cleaner and a storeman, making surveillance a probability and gender seclusion difficult. The design and finish of these toilets not only deters the proliferation of graffiti through being graffiti-resistant but it also deters graffiti writing in the first instance because the environment it produces is not conducive to social gatherings. The rearrangement of space, materials, and bodies through changes in toilet design therefore has a subtle but penetrating effect on the cultural processes which produce girls' toilet graffiti. It degrades the sociability of the space and in the process redefines the function of the female public toilet as purely biological.

The SRA's technological strategy is doubtless the product of a genuine concern with the appearance of their toilets, rather than with what happens in them. Its impact on the cultural practices of girls who use the toilets in a social way does not appear 'intentional'. But although it is not a conspiracy, and although questions of intention are irrelevant, it is nevertheless a banal and insidious exercise of power, because it appears neutral, as if on behalf of the 'public', and invisible, as if it happened naturally.

I will finish by analysing how three dominant meanings interpreted from inscriptions in public female toilets fit into broader relations of social

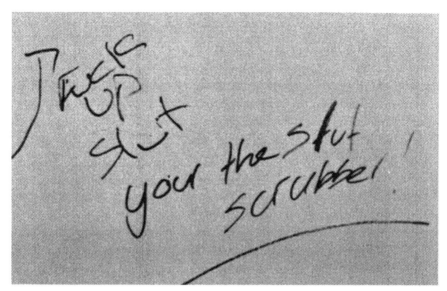

Figure B

inequality. The first analyses the construction of a 'slut' as the signifier of a 'bad girl'; the second examines 'love graffiti' and the construction of boys as romantic objects; while the third discusses the meaning of friendship graffiti in relation to girls' cultural networks.

The term 'slut' does not here refer to its literal meaning in male discourses as a female who copulates with many male partners. The criteria for branding a girl a 'slut' are obscure and arbitrary. Cowie and Lees found in a study of English girls that the label was applied to girls who wear 'sexual' clothes, dress, act, or walk the wrong way, and hang around with too many boys, or with the wrong sort of boys or the wrong sort of girls, or with someone else's boy (Cowie and Lees, 1983 : 20). Very rarely was the term used to imply a strict literal interpretation.

The term slut not only dominates the language expressed in girls' toilet graffiti (see Figure B) but was found by Lees in her study of adolescent girls to be the commonest insult by both girls and boys to tarnish a girl's reputation (Lees, 1986 : 31). It always refers to other girls, not to boys. It is about the exercise of social power and the regulation of gender relations between girls, and between girls and boys. This argument is illustrated with the example of Kathy, who attended the school where the interviews were conducted.

'KATHY IS A SLUT TRUE SUCKS DRIED SPERM' and variations of it appeared on the walls, stairs, and toilets of this high school. On a superficial level Kathy is being degraded for her alleged sexual practices. However, when I asked Kathy's female peers in the school why they wrote this piece of graffiti, the story turned out to be complicated. Helen, Kathy's best friend, had written most of it earlier that day after they had an altercation calling each other 'sluts'. Kathy ran away and locked herself in the toilets for two hours. She was therefore inaccessible during the time of the group interview to tell her side of the story. Meanwhile Helen successfully lobbied their peers with tales of prostitution, fucking her cousin, fucking dogs, in fact 'fucking anything with two legs' as Helen put it. Yet the real source of conflict between these two friends remained obscure.

Kathy is dehumanized by the group. Helen interjects, when asked why boys aren't sluts, 'We're not talkin' about boys, we're talkin' about Kathy.' Kathy is symbolic to all girls who fall out of favour with their peers; she is being constructed as a 'bad girl'.

The finale to the argument exploded when Helen screamed, 'She is a slut. I went up to her and said what did you say to Jenny and she started shakin' and that's what you call a slut, a proper slut.' It is finally apparent that the reason for calling Kathy a slut bears no relation to her alleged or actual sexual behaviour. Kathy is a proper slut because she shook when Helen questioned her about her betrayal of loyalty. What is important about this is its clear demonstration that the label 'slut' is entirely arbitrary. It is not being applied to describe or comment upon Kathy's actual sexual practices. It is being used to wield power within their group.

The phrases, 'FUCK UP SLUT', 'YOU'RE THE SLUT SCRUBBER', 'RIGHT YOU SLUTS I WILL FIGHT YOU PERSONALLY', 'ALL SCHOOL GIRLS ARE SLUTS', 'KIM AND SARAH ARE SLUTS', and 'MADONNA IS A SLUT', are just a few examples found and photographed in female public toilets. The prevalence of the word suggests that it is very influential in the lives of teenage girls.

The world 'slut' is part of an ideology which distinguishes good from bad women, but more importantly validates certain social relations based on male dominance. These labels invoke an entire world-view about what is appropriate female behaviour and what is not. By participating in the everyday construction of sluts, girls actually participate in their social formation as subordinated sex objects. In this sense, they are the bearers of a power relation policing their own subordination to a double standard of sexuality. The power relation defined externally by gender inequality is simultaneously exercised locally between women.

Whereas 'slut' graffiti is about the exercise of social power between girls, romantic graffiti is about relations with boys. As an image, 'love graffiti' depicts the construction of boys as romantic objects, and mirrors the rivalry between girls over boys desired as such objects (see Figure C).

Bruner and Kelso found in their study on gender differences in toilet graffiti that romantic graffiti were an almost exclusively female phenomenon, and they quoted a number of other studies spanning twenty years of research with similar findings (Bruner and Kelso, 1980 : 243, 245). The way one girl has assigned particular boys to girls in a piece of toilet graffiti (see Figure C) can be an attempt to control romantic involvements. In this sense boys are represented as objects of possession, although what these girls are negotiating is romance rather than sexual gratification. The significant feature of the text represented in Figure C is that Vicki cannot exist as a subject in her own right. She is represented as the other half of some entity.

Figure C

Even if it is 'no one', the space for a male has to be provided. What is important is that boys are consistently constructed as romantic rather than sexual objects, while a girl's desire for one is simultaneously constructed as natural, asexual, and imperative to her identity as female.

Tamie's graffiti photographed at intervals over a six-month period further illustrates the point. Tamie is an active graffitist of the Stanmore railway station toilets, and although she has recorded feelings and moods about her relationships with female friends Tamie's graffiti is dominated by her romantic involvements. The first record of Tamie's graffiti, collected in August 1985, depicts her love for Billy, before she crossed it out and inserted Ian. Later that month, on 29 August 1985, Tamie vows she will love Ian always. However, only two weeks later, on 10 September 1985, Tamie has expressed her love for Corey in the same cubicle. Two months later, this graffiti was found to be scratched out, presumably by Tamie. 'TAMIE HATES COREY' then appears in the subway tunnel to this railway station, some time during the first two weeks of November 1985. On 4 November 1985, Tamie recorded her love for Deano in a different toilet cubicle at the same railway station.

Tamie's graffiti is a good indication of the way girls' lives are influenced by a contradictory heterosexual 'love' and 'romance'. Love is meant to be lasting, based on fidelity and monogamy, but it is blatantly obvious to girls like Tamie that 'love' is transient and boys are replaceable. Love is not special, even though it is supposedly 'always for always'. This contradiction is apparent in the graffiti texts of other young women who write on toilet walls. Tamie's type of graffiti, although it undermines the notion of lasting love and can therefore be interpreted as subversive, is only a marginal characteristic of girls' toilet graffiti.

On first impression, then, this type of girls' toilet graffiti about relationships and romance seems to rule out any alternative to the feminine ideal of the heterosexual but virginal girl always hopelessly 'in love'. The only alternative is to be a 'slut'. Any notion of boys being erotically desired is virtually absent in these graffiti texts.

This bleak interpretation of the meaning of girls' toilet graffiti is not, however, the whole story. Graffiti in women's toilets also has a softer side, one which reveals the support networks, intimacy, and genuine caring between women, often over-romanticized by feminists. An American study of gender differences in toilet graffiti found that women's writings were predominantly either of this kind or the typical romantic sort. The authors came to the conclusion that 'the underlying meaning of female restroom graffiti is that they express the co-operation of the dominated and reflect the strategy of mutual help employed by those in a subordinate state' (Bruner and Kelso, 1980 : 249). The image in Figure D is a good example of what Bruner and Kelso mean by advisory graffiti. These photographs, taken from the cubicles of Stanmore railway station, depict an interaction between three girls, Sandra, Tamie, and Christine (Kitty). Sandra's initial message read, 'GOOD-BYE TO ALL YOU FUCKERS AND SLUTS UP THE CROSS, SANDRA'. Kitty comforts Sandra, 'DON'T WORRY AS WE ARE ALL FRIENDS WITH YOU NOW. OH YEAH SANDRA YOU BETTER THANK TAMIE AS SHE STOPPED EVERYBODY FROM TOWN & THE CROSS FROM BASHING YOU. SEE YA! LUV CHRISTINE (KITTY)' (see Figure D). Tamie has also left a note for Sandra: 'HI SANDRA, TAKE CARE LUV ALWAYS TAMIE XXX' immediately next to Kitty's. Tamie and Kitty are dealing with a real problem in their peer relations in attempting a reconciliation with Sandra. The toilet wall has provided a convenient, non-threatening, but effective way of communicating with her. The three girls seem to be operating on two assumptions: first, that this railway station toilet works as a social place where communication can be conducted; second, that toilet graffiti is a meaningful form of communication for the negotiation of peer relations.

The present study, like others (Wales and Brewer, 1976 : 120), found disproportionately more examples of 'advisory graffiti' in toilets with a middle-class clientele. Campus toilets were exemplary in this respect. Conversely, toilet graffiti found in shopping centres, parks, and railway stations of working-class suburbs in Sydney, whose audience and authors one would expect to reflect the constituency of the neighbourhood, expressed predominantly romantic or derogatory messages. 'JENNY LOVES TIM' and 'SARAH IS A SLUT' were typical examples. There was some evidence of advisory graffiti, like the interaction between Sandra, Kitty, and Tamie, but objectively this sort of graffiti is not significant in the toilet etchings of working-class girls.

More prevalent in the toilet graffiti of working-class neighbourhoods is a simple statement of friendship between two or more girls. Inscriptions of this

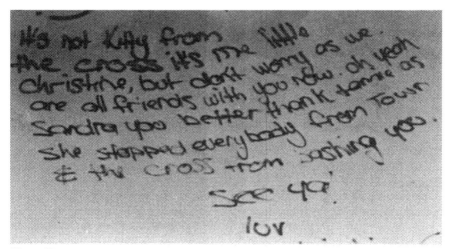

Figure D

sort were found in vast quantities in locations where young and predominantly working-class girls hung around (e.g., western-suburbs shopping centres and railway stations) and were noticeably absent from the toilet walls of Sydney's university campuses. Girls' graffiti can in these instances be interpreted as an ephemeral record of their friendships, or even as an expression of their subliminated sexual desires for one another. Importantly these images of friendships between girls seem to point to the crucial significance of the 'best friend' in the cultural worlds of young women, and working-class girls in particular.

What is important about the best friend is that she can actually displace the need for a boyfriend, making girls' best-friend networks a viable alternative to the dichotomy of romance and slut. The best friend can therefore be the best safeguard against the apparent naturalness and innocence of an ideology which denies women as subjects in their own right. However, as was the case with Helen and Kathy, best friends can also be the perpetrators of an oppressive division of girls into 'good' and 'bad'. The contradictory basis of best-friend relationships itself is what often fuels tension between girls, and so frequently becomes the subject of girls' toilet graffiti. Best-friend packages are neither simply oppressive nor simply supportive; they are problematic and contradictory.

Notes

1 Predominantly working-class areas of the Sydney Metropolitan Region.
2 An inner-western suburb of the city of Sydney which mostly houses working-class and ethnic minority populations.
3 Newington is an elite private boys high school in Petersham. Stanmore railway station is closer to Newington than the Petersham railway station.

References

Amsden, J. (1979), 'Historians and the spatial-imagination', *Radical History Review*, 21, pp.11–30.

Aurban, T. (1986), 'Extra staff hired to fight train violence', *Sydney Morning Herald*, 2 June, p. 9.

Bergala, A. (1984), 'The Photo and its discourse', trans. Theo van Leeuwin, *Australian Journal of Cultural Studies*, 2, 1, pp. 108–14.

Berger, J. (1972), *Ways of Seeing*, London: British Broadcasting Corporation and Penguin.

Boys, J., Bradshaw, F., Darke, J., Foo, B., Francis, S., McFarlane, B., Roberts, M. (1984), *Making Space: Women and the Man-Made Environment*, London: Pluto.

Bruner, E. M. and Kelso, J. P. (1980), 'Gender differences in graffiti: a semiotic perspective', *Women's Studies International Quarterly*, 3, pp. 239–52.

Castells, M. (1975), 'Advanced capitalism, collective consumption and urban contradictions: new sources for inequality and new models for change', in Lindberg, L. N., Alford, R., Crouch, C., Offe, C. (eds), *Stress and Contradiction in Modern Capitalism*. Massachusetts: Lexington Books.

Cowie, C. and Lees, S., (1983), 'Slags or drags', *Feminist Review*, 9, pp. 17–31.

Foucault, M. (1977), *Discipline and Punish*, trans. Alan Sheridan, London: Penguin.

Lees, S. (1986), *Losing Out: Sexuality and Adolescent Girls*, London: Hutchinson.

McRobbie, A. (1978a), 'Working-class girls and the culture of femininity', in Women's Study Group (eds), *Women Take Issue*, Birmingham: Centre for Contemporary Cultural Studies.

McRobbie, A. (1978b), *Jackie: an Ideology of Adolescent Femininity*, Birmingham: Centre for Contemporary Cultural Studies.

McRobbie, A. and Nava, M. (eds) (1984), *Gender and Generation*, London: Macmillan.

Otto, D. (1982), 'Common ground? Young women subcultures and feminism', *Scarlet Woman*, 15 (Spring), pp.3–8.

Sontag, S. (1977), *On Photography*. U.S.A.: Penguin.

State Rail Authority of New South Wales (1985), *Annual Report, 1984/5*.

Thomas, C., (1980) 'Girls and counter school culture', *Melbourne Working Papers*, Victoria: University of Melbourne.

Wales, E. and Brewer, B. (1976), 'Graffiti in the 1970s', *Journal of Social Psychology*, 99, pp. 115–23.

Wilson, P. and Healy, P. (1986), *Graffiti and Vandalism: A Report to the State Rail Authority of New South Wales*, Canberra: Australian Institute of Criminology.

Women and Geography Study Group (1984), *Geography and Gender*, London: Hutchinson in association with The Explorations in Feminism Collective.

Women's Co-ordination Unit, New South Wales Premier's Department (1986), *Girls at Risk: Report of the Girls in Care Project*, Sydney: Government Printers.

TERRY THREADGOLD

TALKING ABOUT GENRE: IDEOLOGIES AND INCOMPATIBLE DISCOURSES

W hen Derrida (1980) said that one 'cannot not mix genres', he was taking up a position which is barely compatible with that of what has been labelled in a recent publication (Reid, 1987) in Australia 'the genre school'. This group of people who are all systemic-functional linguists have been making important and interesting interventions into the pedagogic arena in Australia, using methodologies and ideas that are derivative of, but not necessarily the same as, those of Michael Halliday. Their interventions have aroused both dedicated support and fierce opposition. Other Australian Hallidayans, like myself, whose status as 'linguists', because of their simultaneous positioning in the field of general semiotics, post-structuralism, and social theory, is often questioned in this context, have been working in other ways to extend and broaden an essentially Hallidayan base so as to take the Derridean, and the systemic-functional approaches of linguists like Martin (1985) and Hasan (1986), and a number of other approaches, into account (Birch and O'Toole, 1988). Much of this more broadly based work centres around genre – the many different ways in which it is defined, the things it can and cannot account for, and current attempts in other fields to address the same problems in different, or more complex ways.

There are a number of quite disparate enterprises which presently use the term genre. I shall attempt here only to present the broad outlines of the currency of the term. The generic concepts of the linguists of the 'genre school' in Australia are derived from work in ethnography (Hymes, 1974) and sociolinguistics (Labov, 1967, 1972), often by way of other linguistic uses of the term (Longacre, 1974; Stankiewicz, 1984), and are related to Halliday's original work on register (1978). The use of the term in these areas seems to be the result of an attempt to transfer notions of genericity with a long history in classical rhetoric (Russell and Winterbottom, 1983), and thus in pedagogic and literary contexts (Hauptmeier, 1987), to the analysis of non-literary, but often still pedagogic, processes of textual production. Thus there has been work on curriculum genres (Christie,

1985), expository genres (Martin, 1985), mother-child interaction (Hasan, 1986), service encounters (Ventola, 1979), ritual insults (Labov, 1972), non-literate text-types (Bauman and Scherzer, 1974), everyday forms of talk (Goffman, 1981), and so on. In much of this work genre is conceived of largely as a schema for action, a recipe for producing a text, as in the classical *dispositio* of the rhetorical handbooks and text-books of the medieval and later periods (Howell, 1956). While the social functions of these text-types are always implicit in this work, genre tends to be treated as an autonomous formal characteristic of texts and its ideological and institutional aspects are dealt with only rarely (Poynton, 1985).

In the literary context itself, the use of the term genre has a venerable and chequered history. The most recent attempts to classify, label, and taxonomize literary text-types in these terms are those of Fowler (1982) and Rosmarin (1985), while Colie's work has been much more than taxonomizing and has involved a real exploration of the function of genre in reading and writing practices in an historical context (1972). Other recent work shows the influence of ethnographic and linguistic as well as semiotic approaches to these questions (Van Dijk, 1985).

Often interacting with these kinds of approaches is the more socio-historically based work on genre of the Russian formalists (O'Toole and Shukman, 1978), recent Russian semiotics (Lotman *et al.*, 1975), the Prague school (Vodicka, 1964), and Bakhtin/Voloshinov (1986, 1930). None of this work is taxonomic and all of it sees genre as related to literary or cultural processes of evolution. Genres here, then, are the causes and the effects of dynamic and changing social processes (Evan-Zohar, 1980).

From all of this work there emerges a more complex picture of the function and evolution of genres than is mostly found in linguistics and ethnography. This involves specifying genre's relations with discursive fields (Foucault, 1972) or subject-matters; its possible textual realizations and the typical media in which it is constructed and transmitted (Schmidt, 1987); its relationships with institutions and power and the social semiotic construction of subjectivity; and the relations it permits/enables/constrains and refuses between readers and writers, textual producers, and receivers. It is generally recognized that genericity is characteristic of not only verbal, but also social, behavioural, bodily, environmental, and visual 'texts', for example, and that all of these complex semiotic processes ('languages') interact in the daily business of social meaning making.

These kinds of accounts of genre are also found (in all of the forms enumerated above) in film theory (Grant, 1986), and in analyses of popular culture or 'genre fiction' (Rosenberg, 1982; Radway, 1987; Kress, 1988). Much of this work has also involved post-structuralist, deconstructive, and feminist attempts to unsettle the system-process, type-token dichotomies and the a-social taxonomic autonomy of western epistemologies of genre (Poynton, 1985; Cranny-Francis, 1988; Threadgold, 1988b). Bakhtin's dynamic accounts of genre and his re-location of genre in the non- or extra-literary world have been very influential here and have contributed, along with Derrida's fluid and complex conceptualizations, to an understanding of the essentially intertextual, processual, heteroglossic, and always only probabilistic nature of that which we recognize and name as generic. In this context, too, the idea of rigid boundaries between genres, that is of genres that are in some sense 'pure' and do not mix, has also been radically questioned. Hence Derrida's conviction, quoted at the outset, that 'we cannot not mix genres'.

It is then against this backdrop of multiplicity and contestation with respect to the nature, existence, importance, and dangers of generic thinking about genre, that the 'genre school' in Australia has to be seen.

The current debate about the validity of generic approaches to the teaching of writing, and to teaching practices in general, in the Australian context, is an extremely interesting phenomenon in its own right. It is actually a part of a much wider socio-historical process: and it participates in 'ways of speaking' (Whorf, 1956), and of knowing and believing, that are themselves involved in both the maintenance and transmission *and* the deconstruction (i.e., the critical analysis in a specific historical and social context) of what Lyotard (1984) called 'the great cultural narratives' by which and through which we actually construct and at the same time make sense (to and for ourselves) of our everyday and institutionally ratified worlds. Seen in this light the apparently incompatible positions of Martin (1985, 1985a), Martin and Rothery (1986), Christie (1984, 1985), Kress (1985, 1987), Dixon (1987), and Sawyer and Watson (1987) make a great deal more sense and can, I think, be very productively and constructively made to work together.

I believe that genre is a fundamental social category/process which demands careful analysis and understanding in the present context. That is why the work on genre of the systemic-functional school of linguists is of crucial importance. However I do not believe that genre is an ideology-free, that is, 'objective' or 'autonomous' scientific (for which here read 'linguistic'), category/process. It therefore cannot be treated in isolation from the social realities and processes which it contributes to maintaining (and could be used to subvert); nor can it be seen as separate from the people (the agents of reality maintenance and change) who 'use' it, analyse it, and then, perhaps, teach others how to use it.

That is why those who criticize the current systemic-functional approaches to genre must also be heard and listened to: but that is also tantamount to saying that 'linguistics' on its own is not enough. At least, it is not enough if its job is conceived of as that of specifying the bits and pieces (both obligatory and optional) that constitute linguistic categories like 'narrative' or 'expository' genres (Martin, 1985a): and it is not enough if it then imagines that meaning or significance is somehow contained 'within' those categories, constructed as generic schema or flow charts (e.g., Martin, 1985a; Ventola, 1984), which are seen as a-historical, a-social, and non-ideological (that is 'objective' or 'transparent' (Barthes, 1953:16–17) patterns that can be taught to children without having political and social consequences. It is of the latter that the critics of 'genre-theory' (the educationalists and literary scholars in the debate) have been much more aware than the linguists (Reid, 1987). However neither side in the debate has seen its own participation as framed, contextualized, and classified (to use Bernstein's 1982 terms somewhat loosely) by an absolutely incompatible set of discourses. 'Discourse' here is again used loosely in a Foucauldian sense to mean those sets of statements which we characteristically 'use' to put together our theoretical stories (Rosen; Steedman). 'Use' is in inverted commas, because these statements are in fact akin to what Whorf (1956) called 'fashions of speaking', and described as those regularly patterned configurations of ways of 'speaking' the world around us that are so deeply ingrained in our consciousness by early processes of linguistic socialization (Hasan, 1986) that in fact they 'speak', us while we say regularly and therefore think, thus proving Whorf's point, that we 'use' them.

The discourses I have in mind involve:

(1) what Foucault (1971) called the discourse of humanism and char-acterized as 'everything in western society which restricts the desire for power' (1971:44). The Humanistic discourse involves the difficult concepts of individualism, freedom, choice and law;

(2) the related discourse of empiricism with its equally difficult concepts of the 'knowing' scientific subject (who can observe objectively), the consequent construction of subjectivity and objectivity as opposite and separate, and the rigid 'framing' of the science/humanism opposition that goes with that; plus the framing and classification of the disciplines as we know them, as separate and autonomous enterprises, constructed as logical systems on the basis of exclusion (hence a Saussurean 'linguistics' that sets itself up as excluding the social and historical aspects of a social theory);

(3) the discourse of Romanticism, engendered in part by both of these, with its even more contradictory denial of constraints, systems, norms, and laws and its valorization of individual creativity and freedom.

And if that degree of complexity and incompatibility were not enough, there are what I shall call the 'semiotic' discourses that impinge upon and run through all of these, the characteristic and recurrent configurations of statements which construct stories (theories) about what meaning is and how it works. Thus, for the empiricist, meaning is unproblematic. It is 'contained' in forms and able to be transmitted through them like water through pipes (see Reddy, 1979). The same general idea is constantly re-constructed and transmitted by the discourse of humanism. The ambigui-ties of the freedom, choice/law problematic can only be apparently resolved if meaning can be fixed, located, in 'forms' and identified. Then one can 'know' what one *has* to do. And these 'ways of speaking' impinge upon even a linguistics that *recognizes* the fallacy of what Reddy (1979) called such 'conduit models of meaning', particularly when it isolates *genre* as a 'linguistic' category from the social processes which produce it and which it then reproduces in turn.

On the other hand, the romantic discourse separates form from content, liberating meaning from its 'pipe', valorizing content over form (which becomes a 'dirty' scientific word – viz. formalism, structuralism, etc.) thus reconstituting the science–humanism split and prizing polysemy and ambiguity over fixity of sense. This produces the Romantic ideology of the aesthetic text as that which escapes all systems and the idea of the individual need, and ability, to mean in ways that are seen as totally 'free' of social and historical constraint. And that is not yet all. There is another discourse about the nature of meaning or more generally of language which pervades all these others and, as Halliday (1979) has pointed out, has been with us in the west since Aristotle. Halliday has characterized this as a concentration, in western attempts to describe language, on what he calls the 'particle'-like structure of language at the expense of what he has called its 'wave'- and 'field'-like aspects: these, he argues, always operate simultaneously with the particulate structure of language. That is, our theories of language have concentrated on breaking linguistic structure down into hierarchies of constituent parts (that is the particles of which it is constructed) and in seeing language as operating through a synthesis of these constituents into more and more complex units. Thus words into phrases, phrases into clauses, and so on; and there is then a corresponding emphasis on the referential or representational nature of meaning: for each of the constituents ('particles') is then seen as 'referring' to or 'representing' an appropriate 'bit' of reality in a one-to-one, absolutely unproblematic way.

There are shades here of the seventeenth-century nominalist doctrines (Wilkins, Hobbes, Locke, etc.) which Swift satirized in *Gulliver's Travels* when he depicted philosophers as having to carry bundles of 'things' around on their backs so as to be able to 'represent' reality without the problematic mediating effect of linguistic forms; but this is also the basis for the link between signifier and signified in de Saussure's entirely inadequate (see Eco, 1976) characterization of the linguistic sign as a 'bit'/particle of language (form) representing, referring to, a 'bit' of reality.

Such theories of language and meaning, as Halliday (1979) points out, ignore the wave-like structures of the textual functions of language – its text-forming properties, the kinds of processes Halliday and Hasan (1976) described a long time ago as 'Cohesion': processes which operate in, through, and across constituent structures of the referential type. They ignore also the field-like structures of the interpersonal function – which are mapped onto all of these in ways that do not coincide exactly either with the particle-like patterns of the referential (Halliday's Ideational) function or the wave-like patterns of the textual.

Now, it seems to me that, in concentrating on the description of genres, on 'schematic structures', made up of obligatory and/or optional 'elements', systemic-functional analyses of genre have been doing precisely what Halliday is here describing. That is, they are reproducing the philosophical discourse of referential meaning, and participating in the transmission of a particle-based theory of language. Genres are *not* simply schemas or frames for action. They involve, *always*, characteristic ways of 'text-making' (what in systemic-functional terms we could call mode), and characteristic sets of interpersonal relationships and meanings (reader/writer relationships, and positions of power, writer/text orientations – for example, first person (writer-in-the text), third person (writer-outside-the-text) narrative and so on: tenor in systemic-functional terms) as well as what appear to be restrictions on 'what' can actually be appropriately talked/written 'about' (the referential function or field in systemic-functional terms). Linguistic analyses of genres have had relatively little to say about the first two of these aspects of genre, although they are taken for granted in literary (Fowler, 1982), filmic (MacCabe, 1985), and even some ethnographic approaches to the problem of what genres are.

The reason for this is the inevitable imbrication of linguistics in the discourse of referential meaning. It may not be impossible to see round the corners of Whorf's 'ways of speaking' (as Halliday has somewhere said) but 'ways of speaking' and meaning can make it very difficult to see that one should try to look around corners: even then, it is not easy to unsettle entrenched ways of talking (as Reddy, 1979 has demonstrated). The consequence of this description of genres as if they were simply bundles of constituents to be arranged in a certain order is a failure to see what a multi-functional approach to genre would *have* to foreground, that is, that they are reality-maintaining and constructing processes. In this sense they both construct and are constructed by the typical and socially ratified situation-types that constitute the everyday realities of cultures: but those situation-types and their corresponding genres cannot be where the process begins and ends (which is what Martin's (1985a) and Hasan's (1985) views would both suggest).

They are already enmeshed in a whole web of social, political, and historical realities. The relevant questions have to be much 'higher' (in Halliday's terms), or, to remove the vertical metaphor, are to be located in the traditional (since Saussure) 'outside' of linguistics, in politics, social theory, and history (for example). What we need to know is how institutions and institutionalized power relationships and knowledges are both constructed by and impose constraints on (and restrict access to) possible situation-types *and* genres. We need to know why certain genres are highly valued, and others marginalized. We need to understand the changing history of such valorizations. We need to know why some genres are possible, others impossible, ways of meaning at given points in history. We need to know how and why these factors construct identities for social agents (the people who think they 'use' the genres) and how and why some social agents are able to/willing to resist and others to comply with existing situational and generic constraints (Bernstein, 1982). For it may be a truism, but while you can lead a horse to water, you cannot make it drink: and even providing equal access to situation-types and genres does not always produce equal results. We need to know how processes of socialization and education are tied up in systematic and important ways with the possible situation-types, genres, and meanings of a culture – that is with the framing and classification processes Bernstein has called 'context' (see also Brice-Heath, 1985; Hasan, 1986).

Finally we need to know if genre is enough to explain the enormous complexities involved in these questions about the construction, transmission, and potential changing of social and cultural realities. Are there other kinds of 'organizations of meanings' – to put it roughly – which contribute? I believe there are. The 'discourses' I have already identified in this paper are among them. Such discourses are highly patterned, systematic, and regular, but they can be realized in many different generic forms: in, for example, the linguistic analysis of genres, in literary critical accounts of these linguistic analyses, in pedagogic texts on reading and writing practices and so on. And then there are the 'theoretical stories' I have alluded to above, and the everyday 'stories' (Hasan, 1986) which involve systematic, regular, and patterned sequences of elements of these discourses which we 'use' to 'make sense' of our worlds and to construct them. These 'stories' too turn up in many different generic forms – in novels and newspapers, in poems and talk between parents and children, in films and Mills & Boon romances and on television, in news reports and soap operas. They are akin to what Roland Barthes called 'mythologies' (1973). But neither they, nor discourses, are the same thing as genres and genres themselves are not just 'schema' – they involve the other kinds of meaning, characteristic of the interpersonal and textual functions of language described above. These will have to be clarified and described for specific genres if we are to teach genres effectively.

There is every reason to believe that writing effectively depends on the discourses and the stories as well as the genres – so we will have to teach those too if we want to teach what it is we do when we read and write. Even more so will we have to teach them if we want to make it possible for social agents to see round the corners of the 'fashions of speaking' that *are* the lexico-grammar of texts, in ways that will enable them to change the situation-types or the genres, and unsettle current framing and classification processes and their associated voices and messages (Bernstein, 1982).

However to ask any of these questions of genre, to relocate genres in this fashion, is immediately to see genres as among the very processes by which dominant ideologies are reproduced, transmitted, and potentially changed. To teach genre, then, is not an academic exercise, insulated as academia always likes to see itself, and removed by the culture/politics dichotomy (Batsleer *et al.*, 1985) from political and social realities. To teach genres, in their existing intertextually ratified forms, is to contribute to the further entrenchment of existing ideologies and cultural and social practices and power relations. It is *also* to provide access to power and knowledge for those who, in a world where such access is never equal, might otherwise be denied it. It is thus also to unsettle the framing and classification procedures which deny or restrict such access. And *there* is the contradiction. The teaching of genre is potentially *both* conservative/reactionary *and* revolutionary.

To make genre, discourse and story 'visible' by teaching them is potentially to provide the means if not the certainty of subversion and change. It is to provide the impetus for looking around the corners of the grammar, for unsettling the dominant 'ways of speaking' (viz. the recent effects of the feminist discourse). It is, to use Eco's (1976:29) phraseology this time, 'to intervene in the process of semiosis' – something which cannot but result in change.

But this cannot happen until the analysis and description of genres takes into account the difference between schematic (i.e. descriptions of activity structures) and multi-functional approaches and proceeds to teach genre as product *and* social process (Martin, 1985b), as functional and ideological, and in ways that do not take for granted the textual (see Martin, 1983) and interpersonal modes of meaning involved. They too have to be taught if the ideology of genre is to be understood, 'used', and changed; which is why the linguists *and* their critics do indeed argue from incompatible positions but towards a common end.

The contradictory nature of the discourses involved can be illustrated further and briefly by quoting Martin's (1985) definition of genres as 'goal-oriented social processes' (although this is an ethnographic definition originally).

This immediately (despite its reference to the 'social') participates both in the humanist *and* the romantic discourses, with its connotations of individualism and freedom *of* action, freedom *to* act. And yet it is precisely the threat to such individual freedom that is often the basis for the educational response (e.g., Sawyer and Watson, 1987) to the other aspect of Martin's position – the formalism, normativeness, and systematicity of the systemic-functional accounts of genres as 'schema'. In this the educational-ists' response is couched in terms of the romantic discourse. The debate is inevitably on shifting ground, constructed in and around contradiction and conflicting discourses, what Bakhtin would have called polyphony or heteroglossia, the many different voices that emanate from the centres and peripheries of the culture.

Such then are the contradictions and the discursive, 'mythological' (stories) and generic resources that constitute the stuff of the debate on genre. Let me summarize what seem to be the major issues and problems that emerge from this.

1 Neither current genre-theory in linguistics nor critiques of such theories are themselves adequately historically contextualized.
2 Descriptions of genres which concentrate on their constituents (the particle/referential approach) in the form of generic schema and ignore their text-forming and social-structure-constructing resources must be justifiably seen as reductive and formalistic, and more important, as inadequate for the teaching of genre to those who do not already have those resources.
3 Genres are not autonomous, objective categories which can be separated from their participation in historical, social, and political processes.
4 Genres are both 'products' *and* 'processes' – 'systems' and 'performances'. Each time a text is produced so as to realize and construct a situation-type it becomes the model for another text and another situation-type. As a model, it functions like a static, finished product or a system according to which new texts can be constructed. Once the constructing begins it

becomes again a dynamic process, a 'performance' which will inevitably change the model with which it begins. This means that we have to teach the interpersonal and textual characteristics of genres, the probabilistic, dynamic aspects of their performance as well as their schematic structures.

5 To produce a text is not just to reproduce a generic model, even an adequately described one. Genres are the socially-ratified text-types available within a community. They are permitted by and reproductive of the socially-ratified and identifiable situation-types of the culture. As such their function is that of both reality-maintenance and reality-change. They provide the possible formats for the construction, combination and transmission or transformation of the discourses, and stories that are the 'other' non-generic intertextual resources (models, patterns located in other texts) for the production of new texts.

If we are to teach textual production (i.e. writing or reading) then, we have to teach genres, discourses *and* stories and we have to teach how it is that these inhibit the performance of other genres, the construction of different discourses and the telling of other stories (Steedman, 1986).

6 Texts are not necessarily formed or produced on the basis of single generic patterns. They may also be multi-generic. These are not random differences. They are historically, socially and functionally constrained: and we will need to be able to teach the difference between and the motivations for multi-generic and single genre texts.

To teach genres, discourses and stories is inevitably to make 'visible' the social construction and transmission of ideologies, power relationships, and social identities. As such the teaching of textual production, and of the intertextual processes that the text as written, final product conceals, involves giving access to the resources and thus the power to maintain and/or change existing ideologies, power relationships and identities. Either way, the process is essentially and potentially subversive of existing knowledges and of the existing processes and patterns of permitting, denying or restricting access to these.

7 Intervening in the semiotic process by describing it, making the unconscious and the everyday 'visible', inevitably changes the possibilities of meaning within a community. Performing a genre, because it involves not only a schema and a set of social relationships but also the probabilistic and semogenic or meaning-changing (Halliday) processes of textual production *and* the reproduction of often conflicting discourses and stories and possibly of several genres simultaneously, is *never* the simple reproduction of a formalistic model, but always the performance of a politically and historically significant and constrained social process and involves the potential construction of new genres (Bakhtin, 1986).

Relocating the debate in a wider context

The question of the relevance of detailed linguistic/semiotic analysis of spoken and written texts to educational practice and the terms in which this is currently being debated in Australia (Reid, 1987) is closely related to the whole complex question of the ideology of genre and of literature. By this I mean the ways we speak, write, and think (mean) what a genre, and what a literature, is or might be. Written texts produced in an educational context are highly valued texts (or at least aim to emulate highly valued models) and the most highly valued text in that context is the literary. The ideology of literature then (and of genre in relation to it) contaminates 'fashions of speaking' about written, educational texts, in general.

In order to start somewhere we can begin by situating this problematic within the post-Romantic ideology of 'literature', the genre the Romantic ideology constructs as that which exceeds all genres and is thus paradoxically *not* a genre. It is within this framework that 'generic criticism' becomes a derogatory term (Colie, 1972: 215) and this is of course why to see literature as generic, that is 'highly crafted', with the presuppositions of adherence to a pre-established norm or norms, or even worse as 'constrained' by those norms, not 'free', is a problem. 'Literature', at least in our current historically contingent conception of it, is not supposed to be 'generic', in the sense of 'predictable'. Let me quote Ruqaiya Hasan (1979: my italics) here, because even the discourse of systemic-functional stylistics to some extent maintains this ambiguity:

> It is well to remember that the codification of an artistic convention is the very harbinger of its dysfunctionality. Context predicts the typical; *in art the typical is cliché*. (p. 124)

or again:

> It is obvious that apart from the presence of the artistic code *nothing is determined by it*. (p. 123)

and later:

> the ultimate *control* on the selection of events, entities and interactions in a literary text is from the level of theme. (p. 125)

and

> the *theme is closely related to the ideology* of the community in which the artefact has its existence. (p. 126)

and

> in non-literature the contextual configuration can be used as a predictive device. (p. 121)

In this, Hasan is in accord with the general tenor of theories of literary evolution from the formalists, through the Prague School, to the present. (Tynyanov, 1977; Tomashevsky, 1978). Mukarovsky's (1977, e.g. pp. 32, 35, 49) writings are full of this dialectic between 'esthetic norm formation' (p. 45) and 'a tendency to esthetic unpredictability and uniqueness' (p. 49). A later restatement of it is Umberto Eco's (1976) account of the aesthetic text as multiply overcoded *and* invention or Itamar Evan-Zohar's (1979) account of polysystem theory. But Hasan's statement also participates in a discourse alluded to by Rosmarin (1985:7) who says: 'The dissolution of genres ... began with the Romantics: to be a modern writer and write generically is a contradiction in terms'. That the process and the dialectic between the normative and the aesthetic exists is not here in question. What is at issue is, first, the historical contingency of Hasan's statement and second its applicability to *all* literatures.

Predictability in literature is *only* a problem in *some* periods and indeed the classical periods where it seems to be the *law* were of particular interest to the Prague School (see Mukarovsky, 1977:55 ff.). Even in periods like the present where freedom from generic norms is regularly advocated by practitioners and theorists alike, one has to look more closely at what is actually happening before one can decide that literature is not generically constrained or that what is predictable will necessarily be regarded as cliché. Much in post-modernist art-forms is by now entirely predictable but not yet regarded as cliché and so on. What after all *is* 'freedom' from generic norms but a recognition of the existence of the 'ground' against which 'freedom' is possible.

There is an inherent contradiction here that participates in the dialectic of freedom and control which pervades the discourse on literature and genre and is essentially related to the discourses of humanism, romanticism, and individualism in which all our languages are implicated. Literature, in this view, despite the fact that we need 'to place it in perspective as an instance of a specific artist's work, of a particular genre ... etc.' (Hasan, 1979:121) has to be inherently 'creative' and therefore 'free' of constraints, and yet it is structured and therefore there must be a 'control': but if this is 'ideology' (the 'theme' of the work in Hasan's account) it is surely already a *contextual* control and probably one in which *genre* is implicated, since genres are one of the major means in a social system for maintaining and transmitting the disjunctions between those possible and impossible meanings which keep the social system in good working order. This would also mean that, in some sense, 'theme' *is predictable* from 'ideology'/context and therefore *not free* or unpredictable as Hasan seems to argue.

I do not want to persist with this, since Hasan's most recent work in this area (1985) avoids these contradictions. However, what is happening in her text is not unique, and I should like to explore the problem further.

Many of the issues were raised at an interesting conference on Genre/ Literature in Strasbourg in 1980 and have resurfaced in Rosmarin's book (1985) on *The Power of Genre*. Both the conference and the book are concerned with literary semiotics but the problems are similar to those now surfacing in systemic accounts of genre. Both involve the same struggle with concepts of foregrounding, system, and process, and the languages we have developed to talk about these things.

It is extremely interesting to examine some of these languages. 'We typically strive both to unfold the unique and premeditated particularity of the text of our reading experience and to generalise this particularity, phrasing its explanation in terms not its own' (Rosmarin, 1985:6). The consequent sense of the reduction and distortion of the 'literary' by attempts to systematize it is reflected in Croce's post-Romantic assertion (1972:188): 'All books dealing with classifications and systems of the arts could be burnt without any loss whatever'.

What the Romantic ideology constructed as 'literature' was indeed a 'mixture' of genres, the confusion of all the genres that had previously been delimited by ancient poetics. Schlegel puts it this way:

> Other poetic genres are complete and can now be fully dissected . . . only Romantic poetry is infinite as only it is free . . . *the genre* of Romantic poetry is the only one that is *more than a genre*: it is, in a way, the very art of poetry in a certain sense, all poetry is or should be Romantic. (1986, p. 51; my italics)

The contradiction I have marked here which constitutes Literature as a genre, one genre, *the genre*, in the very act of denying any kind of taxonomic distinction of texts into a hierarchical genre system, *and* asserting that every poem is a genre in itself *and* the result of the mutual opposition of various genres, is what Todorov (1976) and Beaujour (1980) have subsequently referred to as 'the terroristic denial of genre in post-Romantic modernism' (Beaujour, 1980:16). It is, as Beaujour (p. 17) points out, a contradiction which characterizes modern western thinking about kind and genericity, but is much older than Romanticism. It has a certain disciplinary basis not unrelated to the late-seventeenth-century science/humanism split, or the more recent social science/natural science dichotomy. Our problems with these concepts, and the extraordinary difficulty we have in discussing them, instantiating/realizing them linguistically, has to do with the incompatibility of at least two contemporary discourses – one of which has a very long history. I am thinking of the incompatibility of the discourse of an empirical poetics and the discourse of the mysticism of the Book, 'Literature'.

The first, which one finds in anthropological and socio-linguistics, ethnomethodology, and systemic-functional linguistics, provides descriptions of genre systems in pre-literate, scribal cultures, or in spoken and written but 'non-literary' contexts (Martin, 1986; Ventola, 1979; Halliday and Hasan, 1985:118)[2] The second is a discourse that is heard in post-Romantic modernism, which demands the overthrow of genres which 'trivialise the Essence of Writing and Desacralise its End' (Beaujour, 1980:16). Genres are mundane, irrelevant, because the only genre that matters is the Book/Literature, and it exceeds all genres.

This discourse has a long ancestry. In the history of western poetics texts of exceptional status have always been regarded as being beyond genre. This is commonly an argument made, for example, both about Homer and about the Bible.

Thus descriptive poetics has been forced to deconstruct two myths, the contradictory discourses of the original unified, coherent text harbouring *all* genres (Homer for example) and the fervently held belief in the *non*-generic nature of sacred revelation (the Bible).

This has had an interesting, and contradictory consequence, recently pointed to in Renaissance criticism (Colie, 1972). Descriptive poetics has placed a correspondingly high emphasis on the singularity of genres, that is their coherence, their obligatory elements, their separateness from one another, and this discourse blends with the Romantic discourse of the genre of literature, what Beaujour (1980:19) calls the illogical attempt to construct an extra-systemic genre as an 'extraterritorial space ... for hieroglyphic writing and interpretations'. Thus the Renaissance concept of *genera mixta* (Colie, 1972:216, n. 10) has become an 'ugly name'. This has meant that the notion of a generically mixed text cannot be countenanced in modern criticism of a kind of poetry that was written in a period when *genera mixta* was, according to Colie, a structural prerequisite in the writing of the texts. The texts therefore are not characterized by the kind of coherence or foregrounding expected by critical readers looking for the single, unique genre, and the many readings of such texts to which Colie's work points are simply themselves incoherent, incompatible as a result.

There is a tendency for current work in systemic linguistics to participate in this discourse, in always seeking to equate 'text' with 'genre' on a one-to-one basis (Hasan, 1985) and making a strict separation between the 'synoptic' or systemic parts of texts and the 'dynamic' or non-systemic parts (Martin, 1985). It is the spatial ordering and linearity of the argument that will I think turn out to be problematic, for it takes no account of the possibility of mapping several generic structures onto a single wording, a kind of simultaneity of realization which is not incompatible with Halliday's view of language as social semiotic (1978).

As Beaujour again points out (1980:19) the judaic separation and segregation of Scripture and other writings which was later replayed as a distinction between Latin and the vulgar tongues, priestly tongues and lay languages, was reinstated by the post-Romantics as an opposition between the vulgar literatures and Ordinary Texts, between the literary and the non-literary, as an attempt to counteract the movement towards equality which accompanies the removal of the sacred. Hence the impossible claim of the Literary/the Poetic to a universal genrehood which is non-systemic and the tying of discussions of the poetic to a rhetoric of secrecy, enigma, and obscurity, which always leads those who wish to believe in the myth of revelation and the poet as its medium, to reaffirm that the Book/'Literature' denies to genre 'the power to assign its place and determine its form' (Beaujour, 1980:17).

As is so often the case, Derrida (1980:204) has managed to articulate the paradoxical position that these contradictory discourses of necessity construct with respect to literature and genre: but he also articulates, more clearly than most, the problem with which we are faced and which gives rise to the contradictions in the first place.

Turning the question on its head, Derrida (1980:204) asks: what if it were impossible 'not to mix genres'. 'What if there were, lodged within the heart of the law itself, a law of impurity or a principle of contamination'. Attempting to describe this principle, and to account for the well attested sense we have that not everything in literature (see the Prague school,

Halliday, Hasan) or indeed in non-literary texts (Martin, 1986, argues that ideology is what register and genre can't account for) is constrained by genre, Derrida declares with characteristic pun, metaphor, and paradox that:

> All these disruptive 'anomolies' are *engendered* (my italics, the English does not preserve the French pun) – and that is their common law, the lot or site they share – by *repetition*. One might even say by citation or re-citation (re-cit), provided that the restricted use of these two words is not a call to strict generic order.

Thus it is the very business of 'citing' the genre (the type/token relationship) which produces that which is not generic. But that is not all:

> A citation in a strict sense implies all sorts of textual conventions. . . . There would be no cause for concern if one were vigorously assured of being able to distinguish with vigor between a citation and a non-citation – a *recit* and a *non-recit* or a repetition within the form of one or the other.. . . . What is at stake, in effect, is exemplarity and its whole *enigma* – in other words, as the word enigma indicates, exemplarity and the recit which works through the logic of the example. (p. 205–6)

It is not only that in the repetition which is generic there is inevitably a recontextualizing and resemanticizing which produces 'degenerescence' or generic change, but that the same example/token of the generic type inevitably carries with it other less easily recognized marks of repetition, quotations/citations from other contexts, other discourses, other genres, which already exceed the genre with which we began. This is the sense in which we cannot 'not mix genres'. But, at the same time,

> 'if a genre exists (. . . the novel, since no-one seems to contest its generic quality), then a code should provide an identifiable trait. . . . This *re-mark* . . . is absolutely necessary for and constitutive of what we call art, poetry or literature. It underwrites the eruption of *techne* which is never long in coming. . . . This supplementarity or distinctive trait, a mark of belonging or inclusion, does not properly pertain to any genre or class. The re-mark of belonging does not belong. . . .'

> Hypothesis: a text cannot belong to no genre, it cannot be without or less a genre. Every text participates in one or several genres, there is no genreless text; there is always a genre and genres, yet such participation never amounts to belonging. *And not because of an abundant overflowing or a free, anarchic and unclassifiable productivity,* but because of the *trait* of participation itself. . . . The clause or floodgate (*ecluse*) of genre declasses what it allows to be classed. It tolls the knell of genealogy and genericity, which however it also brings forth to the light of day (*engenders*). (p. 212; my italics)

This is precisely the paradox that Martin, Halliday, and Thibault have been grappling with in systemic theory, using very different metaphors, but similarly struggling to express that process which is the '*trait* of participation' in a language which is structured by and constrains a system/process opposition, such that what cannot be seen as systemic or generic becomes equivalent to 'unclassifiable productivity' or non-generic (my alternative terms are not equivalent either – see Martin, 1985). The difference is that these systemic linguists are working with a theory of realization, which Derrida does not have – but the two approaches can be usefully put together and there are further helpful suggestions and compatibilities in Bakhtin. Bakhtin (1986) saw genre as a process and his work involved a radical critique of formalist approaches to genre 'as a certain constant, specific grouping of devices with a *defined* dominant' (Medvedev, 1978:129). Bakhtin maintains that each reproduction of a text by a subject (and therefore each new example of a generic type) is a new text, a new performance, an event. 'A genre is always the same and yet not the same, always old and new simultaneously. Genre is reborn and renewed at every stage in the development of literature and in every individual work of a given genre' (1984:106). Genre is not therefore something that pre-exists texts but something that texts constantly and continually reconstitute: and it is but one of the factors that determine textuality or literary form. The others (Bakhtin, 1981:288)are all tied to the subject who reproduces the text, and the immediate context of utterance. They are the author's profession, class, age, and regional origin. These many factors that interact in the production of texts are the diversifying elements which mean that all examples of generic types such as the novel are ultimately characterized by heteroglossia.

There are problems with this account (Thompson, 1984) but its ultimate value lies in the recognition of textual and generic reproduction as a performance in which reiteration (or exact replicability) (Eco, 1976) is in fact impossible because of the nature of the reproduction *as event*, performance.

In systemic linguistics there are those who have made the conceptual leap beyond the product/process, schema/performance, synoptic/dynamic systems dichotomy, apart from Halliday himself (1982). Work on probabilistic grammars which suggests the partial independence of the intratextual lexico-grammar from more global constraints and work on intertextuality which shows how the syntagm/paradigm opposition begins to break down when we are dealing with performance or what Martin would call dynamic systems begins to make this leap. It is interesting that some of this work has been very much influenced by Bakhtin. What is intriguing, but not surprising, if we remember the 'Whorfean paradox' (Silverstein, 1979:234) is that having constructed the fiction of well-defined synoptic systems we are now forced to 'escape' them or to see texts as doing so, in order to explain the dynamic processes which are the only realizations of such systems: thus Halliday (1982): 'the partial *freeing* of the lower level systems from the *control* of the semantics . . .'; Martin (1984): 'Language is to a greater or lesser extent *freed* from its connotative semiotics [in mad talk] . . .'; and Thibault (1984): 'The de-automatization of language allows for the "lower" levels of structural realization (i.e., the lexico-grammar) to be relatively *independent* of *determining* choices made at higher levels of semiotic activity' (p. 103) (my italics).

Genres and normative schema or synoptic systems (as the types of a type-token relationship) are only ever intertextual semantic frames or systems. That is, they are only ever constructed in discourse, in texts as performance, and therefore as syntagmatic realizations. Here their possible elements are constantly recontextualized by the always essentially dialogic structure of the co-text (Thibault, 1984) and by a constantly renewed dialectic of more global contextualizations (that is, the new contexts in which the text is read). Genres and systems cannot therefore have static, fixed values, and the extent to which they are predictive of choices in lexico-grammar is constantly subject to slippage and change within the partially independent area of co-textualization at the lowest lexico-grammatical level. Just as genres globally constrain certain choices, those choices realized in a co-text constantly shift, restructure themselves and thus feedback into the generic process and the socio-semantics by becoming in turn the type for new tokens (Bernstein, 1982, Fig. 10.7, describes the same complex processes).

This is the sense in which I understand Halliday's and Thibault's accounts of the partial independence, and semogenic potential, of the processes of meaning that are characteristic of the lexico-grammatical level of texts as events, as performance. Silverstein (1979:234) puts it this way:

> If 'structure' is a set of (formalizable) patterns according to which 'action' (contextually-situated social behaviour) is interpretable, a so-called synchronic statement (or model) of 'structure' tells us in what respect 'action' remains the same within a social system, in what sense discernible instances of social behaviour remain 'the same' action. What we find, however, when we attempt to apprehend everything in such structural terms (here we return to Whorf's theme of 'indeterminacy') is that 'plus c'est la meme chose, plus ça change'.

Is genre all there is?

Let me outline some of the problems that my attempt to analyse a part of a debate sequence within a Biblical epic about the Fall of Man by Milton (*Paradise Lost*, Book II) forced me to confront.

The first question had to do with genre (Threadgold, 1988a). To start with, Milton claimed to be constructing a new one. How then does one do that and what relationship does the doing have to genres that already exist, since it seemed very clear that he was using well-known genres of many kinds to construct his Biblical epic. The 'text' I had chosen was a written representation of a highly coded form of speech (a debate), a particular genre of debate, and a dialogue, a conversation between a narrative voice and the voice of characters, and between the voices of characters – in an epic poem. And what of this language in which I cannot but write – in what sense do genres 'already exist' and how does one 'use' them – are they not always and only ever textual productions/processes, always the performance tokens of a never instantiated type?

And then there was the problem of adequacy. Did genre or genres explain what there was in this text? The answer was clearly no, as it obviously was for Martin (1986) and Thibault (1984) in their own textual work. Martin resorts to labelling everything not accounted for by genre and register as ideology and Thibault speaks of choices at the lexico-grammatical level 'by-passing' the socio-semantics and selecting directly from the higher-order social semiotic. In my text there was clearly much more – a multitude of systems of ideas and beliefs (coded or overcoded across field, tenor, and mode), social discourses, social heteroglossia, conflicting codes or discourses from generic and other discursive formations which seemed to make it absolutely necessary to specify the 'voices' in the text (Bernstein, 1984) in generic *and* other terms, and to think about the positioning of speaking subjects (readers/hearers, speakers/writers) and coding orientations as questions of framing, access to genres, discourses, and so on. This seemed to involve the need to distinguish between 'genres' and this 'other than genre' and the need to develop some theoretical framework for handling the interdiscursive or intertextual relations that are involved here.

There is clearly, in some sense, a type-token like mapping of whole chunks of discursive material from text to text, rather than from system to text, as our current theoretical languages would have it. It is this text-to-text relationship that has prompted Lemke (1985) and Thibault (1986) to describe these 'chunks' theoretically as *intertextual* 'thematic frames'. What such 'frames', as theoretical constructs, describe, is the semantic potential, at the cultural level, which is available to be realized in textual production (either reading or writing, speaking or hearing). As such, they provide the theoretical means of describing, as part of a social semiotic theory of language, the way in which 'discourses', 'stories', and 'genres' are actually mapped from text to text.

The crucial point is that these intertextual frames are never part of an abstract 'system' (in the Saussurean sense). They are always and only constructed and reproduced in texts as social processes, that is, as events, performances. They 'pre-exist' any particular 'use' only as 'chunks' – familiar, taken-for-granted 'ways of speaking' – in other texts. Thibault (1984) has also pointed out that this is where current views of the operation of syntagm and paradigm in language also break down. They map from one syntagmatic instantiation (the 'frame' realized in a textual process) to another, not from paradigm to syntagm in the Saussurean sense. That is, we do not have to construct the frame again word by word each time.

What seem to be at work here, between texts, are co-variate relations of the type first established for discourse by Halliday and Hasan (1976) and further described by Halliday (1985). What they described were the way meanings are made at the lexico-grammatical level (syntagm) in ways that cut across traditional-grammatical categories and explanations and are always essentially probabilistic. That is we can say (predict) what are the *probable* directions a text may take at this level. Once the text is produced we can retrospectively 'explain' why it took the direction it did but we cannot really know in advance. It is this probabilistic nature of certain kinds of linguistic/semiotic processes that is crucial to the explanation and possibility of change. And these same kinds of processes seem to be working at the cultural level at which intertextual resources for meaning are mapped from text to text (rather like the way, for example, lexical patterns of cohesion or patterns of ellipses or reference are mapped from clause to clause).

It is precisely the details of these processes, at both the discourse (lexico-grammatical) and cultural (intertextual) levels that we will have to understand if we want to teach genre as part of a social semiotic theory of language in the classroom. It is the probabilistic nature of these processes that we have to grasp and that will mean that we have to find new (not synoptic/static) ways of describing systemicity.

It is not surprising that, in this context, Martin (1985) should have found reference and casual conversation impossible to predict as synoptic systems. What we need here is a different (but to some extent already available in Halliday and Hasan, 1976) understanding of systemicity and of genericity. It will need to be of a probabilistic, not static or formalistic kind.

The question then is what are we going to call 'genre' and what are we going to call its 'other'. Problems of definition here are immense. As Derrida has said:

> It comes as no surprise that, in nature and art, genre, a concept that is essentially classificatory and geneologico-taxonomic, itself engenders so many classificatory vertigines when it goes about classifying itself and situating the classificatory principle or instrument within a set. (1980:208)

One is tempted here to sympathize with Eco (1976) and to call the culture a hypercode and refer to all those processes of global contextualization which work in and through texts as extra-coding and over-coding. Except that there do seem to be different kinds of intertextual coding at work here and they are more various and more systematic that Eco's (1976) deductive and abductive categories will account for.

Let me give an example from my Milton text. It does display a sequence of 'text-types', consisting of opening and closing narrative frames and speeches by characters in a debate sequence within an epic poem. These are graphically, rhetorically, and lexico-grammatically marked and identifiable. However, there is immediately a monologic/dialogic conflict between epic and debate genres, a spoken/written conflict between debate as a spoken-mode genre, and its representation within an epic, a written-mode genre, and a conflict between two apparently contradictory rhetorical genres, that of a deliberative, place rhetoric, and that of a Ramist logic. Both arguably carry the statements of the episteme of order, arrangement and control (Foucault, 1972), but they are ideologically contradictory (inductive vs. deductive) and practically incompatible:

Place Rhetoric	Ramist logic
places	syllogism
(topics)	(if – then; either – or)
taxonomy	argument
(nominals)	(disposition)
parataxis	hypotaxis
(written/periodic sentence)	(speech – oratory)

And yet both are mapped simultaneously onto the lexico-grammar of this text and, as mappings, are embedded within other generic mappings onto the same wordings (the epic for example).

This brings me back from the consideration of world-views and fashions of speaking (stories and discourses) and ways of contextualizing the genres to the consideration of the particular: what is spoken from a specific context by a specific individual. For the simultaneity of all these discourses in Milton's text is not unrelated to the positioning (in discourse) of Milton as writing subject, to the juridico-political, family, marital, educational, and other positionings which construct the speaking subject, determining access to discourses and coding orientations and genres. From this a whole lot more of Milton's text seems predictable, rather than having to be viewed as a momentary 'freedom' from genre or generic norms. (Note that Mukarovsky (1977) always emphasized the importance of the individual and the specific context of utterance as predictive of textual choices, even in literature.)

Much of what is there is certainly not accounted for by those genres with which Milton was ostensibly working or which were coded as literary at the time. Much of it is, like snatches of a conversation, overheard at a distance, little more than a citation/quotation/speaking in/of the voice of the other, other voices, from other discursive formations, other discourses, 'voices' which cut across and through the dominant discourses, contradicting them, potentially destabilizing them. But my point is that they do come from other texts, other semantic frames, other positions. This means that probably very little in texts is absolutely unconstrained or unpredictable in terms of contextualization, but that a normative, synoptic, or monological view of the *process* that is context will never begin to account for a process in which dominant and resistant discourses constantly vie with one another, a heteroglossic process of enormous complexity involving the discourses and stories mentioned above as well as genre.

Let me try to take this complexity in easy steps. First, what is it that we seem to think a genre is? Folk-theoretical and taxonomic accounts are actually very helpful here. In a book called *Genreflecting* (Rosenberg, 1982) subtitled *A Guide to Reading Interests in Genre Fiction* and written by a librarian, we find a fascinating taxonomy of genres, and an equally arresting set of statements about the current 'value' placed on genre. For in some circles 'genre fiction' (with its attendant assumptions that there exists fiction which is *not* generic) is a dirty word (p. 33). What is very clear from Rosenberg's book is that 'genre fiction' is currently equated with 'popular culture' and the reading tastes of 'the common reader' (p. 27) for whom, it is said, 'the reading of genre fiction is an escape into fantasizing' (p. 1), and whose reading is assumed to consist of a mimetic practice of uncritical identification with the world, the characters of the fiction. 'Each reader may choose the desirable worlds or characters, the type of genre, to identify with' (p. 1). Genre fiction readers are 'compliant' readers for whom reading is a recreational pastime.

There is a clear disjunction between this and the view of those variously classed by Rosenberg as middle-class, intellectuals, and librarians who 'are uneasy when confronted with genre fiction and popular taste' (p. 16), who 'look somewhat askance at the types of literature enjoyed wholeheartedly by the common reader' (p. 27), or who, like Richard Hoggart, are prepared to declare that 'The public's self-improvement, not its recreation, is the librarian's first concern' (p. 33). Self-improvement, it seems, derives from a literature, a fiction, which is 'other', which is *not* genre fiction. What is at issue here is a disjunction between literature and what is generic, between what is predictable/generic and what is valuable as literary experience. What is valuable is apparently that post-Romantic 'literature' that exceeds all genres and is thus *not* generic or rather (and contradictorarily) *the* genre *par excellence*. There is a similar disjunction between fantasy and realism, where the former is seen as the negative term, and women, children, and 'the common reader' (who is *not* intellectual, middle-class or a librarian) are equated: 'impelled by omnivorous curiosity, ignoring selectivity, and innocent of critical taste, children read whatever is enjoyed.' Whatever is enjoyed is defined as beloved 'trash' totally 'lacking in literary value', that is, 'genre fiction' (Rosenberg, 1982:27–8).

The list of genres handled by Rosenberg is as follows: Western Thriller, Romance, Science Fiction, Fantasy, Horror. Every genre is capable of multiple realizations. Some we would define in terms of field, others tenor, others mode. For example, the Western seems to be recognizable in terms of the thirty-six themes and types listed in the book – for example, Mountain Men, Wagons West and Early Settlement, Texas and Mexico, Mormons, Railroads, Lost Mines, and so on. Some of the latter categories in the list seem to be merging into other genres (or to be mixed genres), for example, Romance, Picaresque, Comedy, and Parody. But there is clearly a high degree of predictability which is functional in terms of reading, writing, and publishing practices. When we turn to Romance it is the schematic structure of the plot and in some sub-genres, like the Gothic, it is narrator–reader (tenor) relations, aimed at producing terror and fear in the reader, that seem to be the dominant elements. It is interesting that this genre is, for Rosenberg, the one that is hardest to distinguish from literature like Richardson's *Pamela*, or the novels of Trollope, Austen, and the Brontës (p. 128). She makes some attempts to characterize the differences in terms of mode ('quality' of writing) with this and other genres. But what is very clear is that genres *are* recognizable on the basis of a combination of factors which, in Hallidayan terms, involve field, tenor and mode categories, that they are never in fact 'monologic', always dissolving into a variety of sub-genres, and never entirely predictable from stereotypes, although these clearly exist and are very highly coded indeed in the popular culture industry:

> Genre fiction is a patterned fiction. Each genre follows rules governing plot and characters – and abides by some taboos – that are acknowledged by the authors and required by the publishers. . . . The pattern is usually established by one or more sucessful novels that become the prototypes imitated by or emulated by later authors, any of whom may achieve the status of prototypes in a single novel. Manuals for apprentice authors are explicit on the formulas wanted by the publishers. (Rosenberg, 1982 : 17)

Let us be clear here about what we have said so far: to be 'genre fiction' is to be *not* literature in this twentieth-century context. Let us now go back a little. Seeking the origins of 'genre fiction', Rosenberg goes back, first to oral narratives and fairy-tales, then to the ballads and chapbooks of the seventeenth century (p. 28). This historical perspective will however force us to reconsider. As Rosenberg's argument goes, it would appear that in the here and now of *this* social, western, world certain genres and their assumed characteristics are valorized as follows:

high value	*low value*
literature	genre fiction
unpredictability	predictability
realism	fantasy

(it is an interesting point that this would give the historical and social reasons for what systemic linguists working with genre theory have pointed to as the over-emphasis on 'realism' in primary-school writing classrooms).

When we turn back to the seventeenth century these valorizations are turned on their heads. This is because, as Mukarovsky saw so clearly (1964), the genre theory of the Renaissance and the seventeenth and eighteenth centuries, while different at each of these time-points in function, nonetheless was exclusively concerned with the genres that were appropriate to literature. That is, it was the *literature* that was generic. Thus in the Renaissance it was a question of how one might make many genres work to produce a complexity that we have come to call the 'open' text (Eco, 1976; Colie, 1972). By the early eighteenth century it was the question of the law, the discipline of genre, which would produce 'closure', and restrain polysemy, ambiguity, 'eliminate accidentalness and uniqueness' (Mukarovsky, 1964 : 61). This is the body of literary generic law, geneaology, taxonomy, over which Alastair Fowler's (1982) book presides with all the 'vertigines' predicted earlier by Derrida (1980) and with much the same kind of conclusions and methods as are outlined above in Rosenberg's book.

The crucial difference is that what for Rosenberg is the origin of the 'generic' is excluded from the generic by Fowler and the Renaissance and later theorists he is dealing with. Before Romanticism what was Generic was Literature. The rest, the 'popular culture' of political pamphlets, ballads, romances, chapbooks, was not only *not* literature, but also *not* generic; it escaped the law of genre, was excluded by that law, suffering a kind of rhetorical exclusion by inclusion in the classical distinction between high, middle, and low styles. It was seen as a kind of anarchic, free area, unconstrained by the rules of polite society and decorum, by *genre* in fact. It was an area that was not even discussed, therefore marginalized and made invisible. *Genre* has undergone a fundamental shift in positioning – a re-semanticization and revaluation. In the earlier period the characteristics of the literary and non-literary dichotomy were reversed with respect to genre predictability:

high value   *low value*

literature   vs non-literature
genre   vs non-generic
predictable   vs non-predictable

I would suggest that the current attempts to produce a descriptive poetics of genre (which would extend genre to cover the here 'non-generic') and the incompatible poetics of the mysticism of the Book (the post-romantic anti-generic trend in literary criticism) – are still struggling with, enmeshed in these giddy oppositions, and this impossible discourse in which *genre* clearly realizes two absolutely contradictory sets of perspectives and values.

Some brief conclusions

What all this suggests about the debate with which I began is that it cannot be understood, and nor can it get very far, until it is historically and ideologically contextualized in this way. Genre, as currently theorized in systemic-functional linguistics, cannot explain why 'we often feel the need to deny the constitutive power of genre in literary explanation' (Rosmarin, 1985 : 8) precisely because genre as an intertextual category/process is simply inadequate to describe the complexity of what Halliday called the higher order Social Semiotic (1978) although this is what Martin (1984) would seem to argue that generic description does. (He argues that in describing genres one is describing what Malinowski called the context of culture.) But we will never understand why the reaction to the teaching of genres is as it is (see Sawyer and Watson, 1987; Dixon, 1987) unless we do describe and understand that complexity: and that means we have to tackle the problem of understanding what genres are and have been and what their 'other' – discourses and stories – are and have been.

If genre, *per se*, is inadequate to describe the way we produce texts, this does not mean that what *genre* doesn't, can't, explain is anarchic, free, unconstrained. It simply means that we have not yet explored the nature of the text/context relationship enough to be able to say what precisely is predictive of the lexico-grammatical patternings and the possible meanings readers and writers make in and through texts. There is much more to be understood about those elements which seem to 'escape' the system. And an understanding of genre will prove to be central to that enterprise. Not to try to understand those processes, to fall back on the humanistic and Romantic discourses of individualism and creativity, is effectively to maintain the *status quo*, to refuse to provide access for those who need it to those processes by which ideologies are constructed and maintained. Those processes are the discursive capital of the community – its discourses and stories and the genres which shape, structure and transmit them – the resources which constrain and are constrained by the institutions, the knowledges and the configurations of power that constitute the culture. To withhold those resources on the grounds of the arguments of that discourse which more than any other 'restricts the desire for power' by transmitting an ideology of 'subjected sovereignties' (humanism as defined by Foucault, 1971 : 44) – 'the more you deny yourself the exercise of power, the more this increases your sovereignty' – is socially and politically inexcusable. But we are going to have to do a much better job of describing genre before our interventions can really be effective.

References

Bakhtin, M. M. (1986), *Speech Genres and Other Late Essays*, trans. Vern McGee, ed. Caryl Emerson and Michael Holquist, Austin: University of Texas Press.

Barthes, Roland (1953), *Writing Degree Zero*, trans. A. Lavers and C. Smith, New York: Hill & Wang.

Barthes, Roland (1973), *Mythologies*, London and New York: Granada.

Batsleer, Janet, Davies, Tony, O'Rourke, Rebecca, and Weedon, Chris (1985), *Rewriting English: Cultural Politics of Gender and Class*, London and New York: Methuen.

Bauman, Richard and Scherzer, Joel (1974), *Explorations in the Ethnography of Speaking*, Cambridge and New York: Cambridge University Press.

Beaujour, M. (1980), 'Genus Universum', in S. Wever (ed.), *Glyph 7*, pp. 15–31.

Bernstein, Basil (1971), *Class, Codes and Control I: Theoretical Studies Towards a Sociology of Language*, London: Routledge & Kegan Paul.

Bernstein, Basil (1984), 'Codes, modalities & cultural reproduction', in Michael W. Apple (ed.), *Cultural and Economic Reproduction in Education: Essays on Class, Ideology and the State*, London: Routledge & Kegan Paul.

Birch, David and O'Toole, L. M. (1988), *The Functions of Style*, London: Francis Pinter.

Brice-Heath, Shirley (1985), *Ways With Words: Language, Life and Work in Communities and Classrooms*, Cambridge: Cambridge University Press.

Christie, Frances (1984), 'Varieties of written discourses' and 'The functions of language', in *Children Writing: Study Guide*, Geelong: Deakin University Press.

Christie, Frances (1985), 'Curriculum genres: towards a description of the construction of knowledge in schools', paper presented to the Working Conference on Interaction of Spoken and Written Language in Educational Settings, University of New England, November.

Colie, R. L. (1972), 'All in peeces: problems of interpretation in Donne's Anniversary Poems', in P. A. Fiore (ed.), *Just So Much Honor*, University Park: Pennsylvania State University Press.

Croce, B. (1972), *Aesthetic as Science of Expression and General Linguistic*, trans. Douglas Ainslie, London: Macmillan.

Cranny-Francis, Anne (1988), 'Out among the stars in a red shift: women and science fiction', *Australian Journal of Feminist Studies*, 6.

Derrida, J. (1980), 'La loi du genre/the law of genre', in S. Weber (ed.), *Glyph 7*, pp. 176–232.

Dixon, John (1987), 'The question of genres', in Ian Ried (ed.), *The Place of Genre in Learning: Current Debates*, Geelong, Vic.: Deakin University Press.

Easthope, Antony (1983), *Poetry as Discourse*, London: Methuen.

Eco, Umberto (1976), *A Theory of Semiotics*, Bloomington: Indiana University Press.

Evan-Zohar, I. (1980), 'Polysystem theory', *Poetics Today*, 1–12: 287–310.

Foucault, Michel (1972), *The Archaeology of Knowledge*, London: Tavistock.

Fowler, Roger (1981), *Literature as Social Discourse*, Bloomington: University of Indiana Press.

Fowler, A. (1982), *Kinds of Literature: An Introduction to the Theory of Genres and Modes*, Oxford: Clarendon.

Goffman, Erving (1981), *Forms of Talk*, Oxford: Blackwell.

Grant, Barry K. (1986), *Film Genre Reader*, Austin: University of Texas Press.

Halliday, M. A. K. (1978), *Language as Social Semiotic*, London: Edward Arnold.

Halliday, M. A. K. (1979), 'Modes of meaning and modes of expression: types of grammatical structure and their determination by different semantic functions', in *Function and Context in Linguistic Analysis: A Festschrift for William Haas*, (eds), Cambridge: Cambridge University Press.

Halliday, M. A. K. (1982), 'The systemic background', in J. Benson and W. Greaves (eds), *Systemic Perspectives on Discourse*, Norwood, NJ: Ablex.

Halliday, M. A. K. (1985), *An Introduction to Functional Grammar*, London: Edward Arnold.

Halliday, M. A. K. (1987), 'Language and the order of Nature', in D. Attridge, A. Durrant, N. Fabb and C. MacCabe (eds), *The Linguistics of Writing*, Manchester: Manchester University Press.

Halliday, M. A. K. and Hasan R. (1976), *Cohesion in English*, London: Longman.

Halliday, M. A. K. and Hasan, R. (1985), *Language, Context, and Text: Aspects of Language in a Social-Semiotic Perspective*, Geelong, Vic.: Deakin University Press.

Hasan, R. (1979), 'Language in the study of literature', in M. A. K. Halliday (ed.), *Working Conference on Language in Education: Report to Participants*, Sydney: University of Sydney Extension Programme.

Hasan, R. (1985), Part B of Halliday, M. A. K. and Hasan, R. (1985).

Hasan, R. (1986), 'The ontogenesis of ideology', in T. Threadgold *et al.* (eds), *Ideology–Semiotics–Language*, Sydney: S.A.S.S.C.

Hasan, R. (1984), 'The nursery tale as a genre', *Nottingham Linguistics Circular*, 13, Nottingham: Nottingham University Press.

Hauptmeier, Helmut (1987), 'Sketches of theories of genre', *Poetics*, 16, 5 : 397–430.

Howell, Samuel W. (1956), *Logic and Rhetoric in England*, New York: Russell & Russell.

Hymes, Dell (1974), 'Ways of speaking', in R. Bauman and J. Scherzer (eds), *Explorations in The Ethnography of Speaking*, Cambridge: Cambridge University Press, pp. 433–52.

Jackson, R. (1981), *Fantasy: The Literature of Subversion*, London and New York: Methuen.

Kress, Gunther (1985), *Linguistic Processes in Sociocultural Practice*, Geelong, Vic.: Deakin University Press.

Kress, Gunther (1987), 'Genre in a social theory of language: a reply to John Dixon', in Ian Reid (ed.), *The Place of Genre in Learning: Current Debates*, Geelong, Vic.: Deakin University Press.

Kress, Gunther (1988), *Communication and Culture*, Sydney: University of New South Wales Press.

Labov, William and Waletsky, J. (1967), 'Narrative analysis', in June Helm Seattle (ed.), *Essays on the Verbal and Visual Arts*, Washington: University of Washington Press, pp. 12–14.

Labov, William (1972), *Sociolinguistic Patterns*, Philadelphia: University of Pennsylvania Press.

Lemke, J. L. (1985), 'Textual politics: heteroglossia discourse analysis and social dynamics', unpublished paper given at the International Summer Institute for Structuralist and Semiotic Studies, Bloomington, University of Indiana.

Longacre, Robert (1974), 'Narrative versus other discourse genre', in Ruth M. Brend (ed.), *Advances in Tagmemics*, Amsterdam: North-Holland.

Lotman, Ju., Uspensky, B. A., Ivanov, V. V., Toporov, V. N., and Pjatigorsky, A. M. (1975), *Theses on the Semiotic Study of Culture*, Lisse: Peter de Ridder Press.

Lyotard, Jean-Francois (1984), *The Postmodern Condition: A Report on Knowledge*, Manchester: Manchester University Press.

MacCabe, Colin (1985), *Theoretical Essays: Film, Linguistics, Literature*, Manchester: Manchester University Press.

Martin, J. R. (1983), 'Conjunction: the logic of English Text', in J. S. Petofi and E. Sozer (eds), *Micro and Macro Connexicity of Texts*, Hamburg: Helmut Buske.

Martin, J. R. (1984), 'Language, register and genre', in F. Christie (ed.), *Children Writing: Reader*, Geelong, Vic.: Deakin University Press.

Martin, J. R. (1985), 'The language of madness: method or disorder', unpublished manuscript, Sydney: Linguistics Department.

Martin, J. R. (1985a), *Factual Writing: Exploring and Challenging Social Reality*, Geelong, Vic.: Deakin University Press.

Martin, J. R. (1985b), 'Text and process: two aspects of human semiosis', in W. S. Greaves and J. D. Benson (eds), *Systemic Perspectives on Discourse: Selected Theoretical Papers from the 9th International Systemics Workshop*, Norwood, NJ: Ablex.

Martin, J. R. (1986), 'Grammaticalising ecology: the politics of baby seals and kangaroos', in T. Threadgold, E. Gross, Gunther Kress and M. A. K. Halliday (eds), *Semiotics–Ideology–Language*, Sydney: S.A.S.S.C.

Martin, J. R. and Rothery, J. (1986), 'What a functional approach to writing can show teachers about "good writing" ', in B Couture (ed.), *Functional Approaches to Writing Research*, London: Pinter.

Medvedev, P. N. (1978), *The Formal Method in Literary Scholarship: A Critical Introduction to Sociological Poetics*, tr. A. J. Wherle. Baltimore: Johns Hopkins U.P.

Mukarovsky, J. (1964), 'Standard language and poetic language and "The Aesthetics of Language" ', in P. L. Garvin (ed.), *A Prague School Reader on Aesthetics, Literary Structure and Style*, Washington: Georgetown University Press.

Mukarovsky, J. (1977), *The Word and Verbal Art: Selected Essays*, trans. and ed.

J. Burbank and P. Steiner, Foreward by R. Wellek, Yale: Yale University Press.

O'Toole, L. M. and Shukman, Anne (eds) (1978), *Formalism: History, Comparison, Genre*, Colchester: University of Essex.

Poynton, Cate (1985), *Language and Gender: Making the Difference*, Geelong, Vic.: Deakin University Press.

Radway, Janice (1987), *Reading the Romance*, London: Verso.

Reddy, Michael J. (1979), 'The conduit metaphor. A case of frame conflict in our language about language', in Andrew Ortony (ed.), *Metaphor and Thought*, Cambridge: Cambridge University Press.

Reid, Ian (ed.) (1987), *The Place of Genre in Learning: Current Debates*, Geelong, Vict.: Deakin University Press.

Rosen, Harold (no date), *Stories and Meanings*, London: National Association of Teachers of English.

Rosenberg, B. (1982), *Genreflecting: A Guide to Reading Interests in Genre Fiction*, Littleton, Col.: Libraries Unlimited.

Rosmarin, A. (1985), *The Power of Genre*, Minnesota: University of Minnesota Press.

Russell, D. A. and Winterbottom, M. (eds) (1983), *Ancient Literary Criticism*, Oxford: Clarendon.

Sawyer, Wayne and Watson, Ken (1987), 'Questions of genre', in Ian Reid (ed.), *The Place of Genre in Learning: Current Debates*, Geelong, Vict.: Deakin University Press.

Schlegel, F. (1986), *Schriften und Fragmente*, ed. Ernst Behler, Stuttgart: A. Kroner.

Schmidt, Siegfried J. (1987), 'Media genre', *Poetics*, 16, 5.

Silverstein, M. (1979), 'Language, structure and linguistic ideology', in P. K. Cline, W. S. Hanks and C. L. Hofbauer (eds), *The Elements: a Parasession on Linguistic Limits and Levels*, Chicago: Chicago Linguistic Society.

Stankiewicz, Edward (1984), 'Linguistics, poetics and the literary genres', in James E. Copeland (ed.), *New Directions in Linguistics and Semiotics*, Houston, Texas: Rice University Press.

Steedman, Carolyn (1986), *Landscape for a Good Woman: A Story of Two Lives*, London: Virago.

Steedman, Carolyn, Urwin, Cathy, and Walkerdine, Valerie (eds) (1986), *Language, Gender and Childhood*. London: Routledge & Kegan Paul.

Thibault, Paul (1984), 'Narrative discourse as a multi-level system of communication: some theoretical proposals concerning Bakhtin's dialogic principle', *Studies in Twentieth Century Literature*, 9, 1 (Fall).

Thibault, P. J. (1986), 'Thematic system analysis and the construction of knowledge and belief systems in discourse', unpublished manuscript, Italian Department: University of Sydney.

Thompson, John B. (1984), *Studies in the Theory of Ideology*, Cambridge: Polity Press.

Threadgold, T. (1988a), 'What did Milton say Belial said and why don't the critics believe him?' in J. Benson, W. S. Greaves and E. E. Cummings (eds), *Linguistics in a Systemic Perspective*. Amsterdam: Walter Benjamins.

Threadgold, Terry (1988b), 'Language and gender', *Australian Journal of Feminist Studies*, 6 : 41–70.

Todorov, T. (1976) 'L'origin des Genres', *Les Genres du Discours*, Paris: Editions du Seuil, 44–60.

Tomashevsky, B. (1978), 'Literary genres', *Russian Poetics in Translation*, 5 (1978), 52–93.

Tynyanov, J. (1977), 'Dostoevsky and Gogol', in P. Meyer and S. Rudy (eds), *Dostoevsky and Gogol. Texts and Criticism*, Ann Arbor, Mich.: Ardis.

Van Dijk, Teun (1985), *Discourse and Literature: New Approaches to the Analysis of Literary Genres*, Amsterdam: John Benjamins.

Ventola, E. M. (1984), 'Can I help you? A systemic-functional exploration of service encounter interaction', Ph.D. thesis, Department of Linguistics: University of Sydney.

Ventola, E. M. (1979), 'Casual conversation', *Journal of Pragmatics*, 3.

Vodicka, Felix (1964), 'The history of the echo of literary works', in Paul L. Garvin (ed.), *A Prague School Reader on Esthetics, Literary Structure and Style*, Washington: Georgetown University Press, pp. 71–82.

Voloshinov, V. N. (1930), *Marxism and the Philosophy of Language*, trans. L. Matejka and I. R. Titunic 1973, London: Seminar Press.

Walkerdine, Valerie (1983), 'From context to text: a psychosemiotic approach to abstract thought', in M. Beveridge (ed.), *Children Thinking Through Language*, London: Edward Arnold.

Whorf, Benjamin Lee (1956), *Language, Thought and Reality: Selected Writings*, ed. John B. Carroll, Cambridge, Mass.: MIT Press.

▪ REVIEWS ▪

MARTIN MONTGOMERY

I SPY FICTION?

▪ Michael Denning, *Cover Stories: Narrative and Ideology in the British Spy Thriller* (London: Routledge & Kegan Paul, 1987), 168 pp., £6.95.

Cover Stories traces the genealogy of the British spy thriller from its roots in Kipling's *Kim* and Conrad's *The Secret Agent* through to the contemporary work of writers such as Le Carré and Deighton. In this literary history of a popular genre, intermediate landmarks are provided by Erskine Childers, Buchan, H. C. McNeile ('Sapper'), Ambler, Somerset Maugham, Graham Greene and Ian Fleming; and its genealogy is traced in terms of symptomatic readings of exemplary texts, set against a background of social and cultural history. Crucial components of this background are elements such as the Empire (whether in crisis or decline), the Depression, and the rise of consumerism. According to the kind of symptomatic reading undertaken here, spy thrillers project a variety of 'cover stories' with which to negotiate the fissures and cracks in the prevailing ideologies of their time. The work of Buchan and Erskine Childers, for example, provide ways in which 'we can unravel the culture of the social-imperialist crisis' (p. 42).

Indeed, it is as the Empire itself actually unravels that the spy story moves from the margins of popular culture to the centre, where – particularly in the figure of Bond, but also in countless spy stories in newspapers, on film and TV during the 1950s and 1960s – it provides a cover story of 'an era of decolonization and . . . the definitive loss of Britain's role as a world power' (p. 92). Thus, it is possibly on the later proponents of the genre – Fleming and Le Carré – that the strategy of symptomatic reading adopted by Denning can best be illustrated.

In discussing the Bond novels, Denning develops Bennett's re-working of Eco's classic essay, 'Narrative structures in Fleming'[1], in order to isolate three overlapping codes. The first of these is a 'games' code encompassing those myriad examples in the Fleming oeuvre of sporting and game-type contests from bridge and baccarat to golf and a ski chase. (And, at another level, as Eco himself points out, even the narrative itself can be viewed as a kind of game with a predictably structured routine of moves.) The games that Bond plays, however, 'like the liquor he drinks and the automobiles he drives, serve as a kind of guide to leisure' (p. 100). Even here, 'they are not simply guides to consumption, "how-to" books, rehearsals for leisure. Rather they are also redemptions of consumption, an investing of the trivial contests of the fairway with global intrigue' (p. 101).

The second code is one of travel and tourism. Indeed, says Denning, 'the prose of the tourist guide inflects much of these novels' (p. 103). More specifically, however, this code reflects not only the tendency to spend much narrative space depicting the actual travels of Bond (cf. the extended sequence on the Orient Express in *From Russia with Love*); but it also reflects the tendency in these tales to site their action 'along the pleasure periphery' of the tourist belt in settings such as the Mediterranean, the Caribbean, and the Philippines. At one level, these locations provide settings 'for sports, elaborate meals and sexual adventure' (p. 105). At another level, by virtue of his secret service role, Bond is given privileged access to a hidden side of these settings and is able to witness apparently 'authentic' features of local culture far beyond the scope of any tourist.

The third code has been previously elaborated as the sexist code by Bennett,[2] for whom it operates principally in the way that the plots re-position a woman who is 'out-of-place' sexually and politically into a traditional ordering of sexual difference. Denning notes the way in which the emergence of this code coincides with the rise of mass pornography and argues that within the Bond texts it is projected in terms of narratives that are 'structured around the look, the voyeuristic eye, coding woman as object' (p. 109). In the last analysis, he comments, Bond's so-called licence to kill is less important than his licence to look.

In these respects the Bond tales amount to masculinist adventures of classless consumerism – foregrounding the spy as voyeur; Le Carré's work, in contrast, can be read as a lament, a realist interrogation of values in decline, especially those which cohere around the term 'service'. Raymond Williams observed[3] that the idea of service is the great achievement of the Victorian middle classes, deeply inherited by its successors, but ultimately inadequate because in practice with its stress on conformity and its respect for authority it serves 'at every level to maintain and confirm the status quo'. Denning builds on these comments in order to explore the novels of Le Carré as 'cover stories' about white-collar work, seeing them as much in terms of bureaucratic power struggles and everyday office routines as in terms of international intrigue. In these power struggles knowledge is crucial. Key characters operate within organizations marked by hierarchies of information. Interestingly, in the case of Smiley, he occupies a lower position in this hierarchy in each succeeding novel.

Smiley descends the hierarchy of information from the cold executioner of the Circus, the shadowy figure at the end of the tale who epitomizes absolute bureaucratic knowledge, to the middle ground hero of *Tinker, Tailor, Soldier, Spy* who embodies a unified knowledge of the fragmented puppets against that of the total organisation, and finally, in *The Honourable Schoolboy*, to a puppet himself. (pp. 139–140)

In these stories, then, to have knowledge is also to have power. But this also entails the possibilities of betrayal, and Le Carré's work (as in the parallel revelations about MI5 and MI6 from the 1960s onwards) revolves around the hunt for the betrayer, or more particularly 'the mole'. The locus of betrayal is variously a suborned member of the organization or, more critically, the organization itself.

> Thus there is another side to the popular story of Smiley as hero, the successful narrative of white-collar heroics in the Cold War; it is the deeper, more critical tale where the real enemy is the organisation, the organisation that never keeps faith, the organisation that betrays its own men. (p. 140)

And, it might be added, that it is in just these ways that the tales became critical meditations on the middle-class ideal of service. Significantly, Le Carré's latest novel, *The Perfect Spy*, shifts its focus from the mole hunters to the mole himself, so that the narrative object of the earlier tales now becomes the subject with a consequent shift of sympathies. Denning's overall account is quite compelling and his book makes a most important contribution to understanding the historical evolution of the genre. Methodologically, however, his treatment does raise important questions about the reading of a cultural form which I think bear further examination. He is undoubtedly right to ask 'what really is this variant of popular fiction about?'; and he is also undoubtedly correct to argue that it is not really about spying as such. 'Spying', in this fiction, is a flexible metaphor, capable of being inflected in variable and historically specific ways to express, for example, the voyeuristic look of masculinist sexuality, or the politics of the office. Nonetheless, the theoretical basis of these figurative readings is never quite explicit, despite debts to Levi-Strauss, Williams, and Jameson.

Indeed, the notion of 'figuration' is itself a source of problems. Denning tells us, for instance, that the armaments manufacturer so common in the work of Ambler during the 1930s is one of the clearest ways in which 'capitalism has become *figurable*' (p. 74); or that in the work of Maugham and Latimer we may find a 'narrative *figuring* of the writer' (p. 63); or that in Le Carré the upper class mole, Haydon, 'is clearly a *figure* for the ruling class' (p. 124). Thus, it is implied, variously, that a mode of production, a social class and a social role become expressed in the text in terms of some kind of narrative agent – usually a character. At the same time, however, when we are told that the presence of sexuality in the Bond stories 'manifests itself in *figures* of looking, in spying and being spied upon' (p. 112), we seem to have moved into quite a different kind of textual realization (or enactment) of a quite different aspect of the social order, even though the term adopted remains the same. Certainly, 'figure' (with cognate items 'figurable'/'figuration') is made to do a lot of work in mediating somewhat indiscriminately between social milieu and text, without its theoretical status ever being discussed. (Despite its pivotal role in the production of readings, it is not – for instance – listed in the index.) And considering that it is a term which suggests an orientation to textual particulars, there is not a great deal of textual analysis. When citation from particular stories does take place, the text is used most often to support a particular reading in a fairly direct fashion with the words or judgements of a character – as in the following:

> Smiley [thinking of the mole, Bill Haydon] feels 'a surge of resentment against the institution he was supposed to be protecting.' Authority and vocation, the promises of professionalism, are both betrayed. (p. 132)

In short, it does not seem to me that figuration is a fully adequate theoretical concept for mediating between the text and the social milieu, unless we can be more specific in principle about which particular aspects of narrative can be related via the concept to which particular aspects of historically specific social orders.

Indeed, it might be argued that other levels of analysis are required to mediate between historical shifts in the social order and the symptomatic readings of those texts which are seen as constituting exemplars of the genre. On the one hand, it is probably necessary to provide more on the actual production of the genre as a form, partly in terms of its publishing history, but also with particular reference to its commission and marketing as a cultural commodity. And on the other hand – perhaps more crucially – we need to know more about empirical readers and readerships: most basically, 'who reads spy fiction and how, for what types of pleasures?'

Of course, it would not be easy to encompass all these problems within the limits of an introductory survey. And clearly the planned series on Popular Fiction, of which *Cover Studies* forms the first title, is intended to address more specifically some of the issues I have raised above. In the meantime, Denning's book provides an excellent starting point for the study of the spy novel and will also be undoubtedly useful for raising more general issues in the study of popular fiction.

Notes

1 U. Eco, *Narrative Structure in Fleming*, in B. Waites, T. Bennett, and G. Martin (eds), *Popular Culture, Past and Present* (London: Croom Helm, 1981).
2 T. Bennett, *James Bond as Popular Hero*. Unit 21, U203, Popular Culture (Milton Keynes: Open University Press, 1981); also, T. Bennett and J. Woollacott, *Bond and Beyond – The Political Career of a Popular Hero* (London: Macmillan, 1987).
3 R. Williams, *Culture and Society 1780–1950* (Harmondsworth: Penguin, 1961).

Notes on contributors

KERRY CARRINGTON is a sociologist at Macquarie University in Sydney . . . ED COHEN teaches English at Rutgers University, is a member of the TABLOID collective, and has published widely on cultural production . . . JENNIFER CRAIK is a member of the editorial collective of *Cultural Studies*, has written a number of articles on fashion and signification, and teaches media and cultural studies at Griffith University, Brisbane . . . DAVID LEE lectures in linguistics in the English Department at the University of Queensland . . . SALLY STOCKBRIDGE is currently researching her PhD on music video while teaching media and cultural studies at Curtin University in Perth . . . JON STRATTON is the author of *The Virgin Text: Fiction, Sexuality and Ideology*, and teaches sociology at the Darwin Institute of Technology . . . TERRY THREADGOLD is an Associate Professor of linguistics in the English Department at the University of Sydney . . . MARTIN MONTGOMERY is a lecturer on the programme in Literary Linguistics in the Department of English Studies at the University of Strathclyde, Glasgow, Scotland. He is the author of *An Introduction to Language and Society*.

ART HISTORY

Published for the Association of Art Historians by Basil Blackwell

Edited by John Onians (Neil McWilliam from September 1988)

★ Illustrations with almost every article
★ Extensive, in-depth Book Reviews Section, renowned for its excellent coverage of Art History publications
★ Contributions from distinguished writers in the field
★ Articles encompassing the broad spectrum of visual arts and related disciplines from all over the world

Founded in 1978 as the official journal of the Association of Art Historians, *Art History* has rapidly established itself as a leading journal internationally, covering all aspects of the visual arts from prehistory to the present day, including architecture, design and the history of photography and film. It also encompasses other subjects such as religion, archaeology and literature where art has significance and implications.

Art History is essential reading for all art historians in galleries, museums, polytechnics, schools, universities, the commercial world—in fact anyone directly concerned with the advancement of the history of art and design.

Published March, June, September and December

Subscription rates Volume 11, 1988:
Personal: £27.25 (UK) £32.70 (Overseas) US$54.50 (N. America)
Institutions: £43.20 (UK) £46.00 (Overseas) US$73.30 (N. America)

Rates include inland or accelerated surface postage

FOR FURTHER DETAILS, VISIT THE BLACKWELLS STAND

Studies in Latin American Popular Culture

Co-Editors: Harold E. Hinds, University of Minnesota, Morris
Charles M. Tatum, University of Arizona

*An annual English-language journal focusing on the theory
and practice of popular culture in Latin America.*

Subscription rates: $15; Libraries & other institutions: $30; Patrons: $30

Make checks payable to: Send to:
STUDIES IN LATIN AMERICAN   Charles M. Tatum, Co-Editor
POPULAR CULTURE   *Studies in Latin American*
                                                Popular Culture
                                                Department of Spanish & Portuguese
                                                University of Arizona
                                                Tucson, Arizona 85721

For Product Safety Concerns and Information please contact our EU
representative GPSR@taylorandfrancis.com
Taylor & Francis Verlag GmbH, Kaufingerstraße 24, 80331 München, Germany

www.ingramcontent.com/pod-product-compliance
Ingram Content Group UK Ltd.
Pitfield, Milton Keynes, MK11 3LW, UK
UKHW021437080625
459435UK00011B/289